MONEY *and* BANKING
IN IRELAND

TO MY FAMILY

MONEY and BANKING IN IRELAND

origins, development and future

PADRAIG McGOWAN

INSTITUTE OF PUBLIC ADMINISTRATION
ON BEHALF OF THE
STATISTICAL AND SOCIAL INQUIRY SOCIETY OF IRELAND

First published 1990
by the Institute of Public Administration
57-61 Lansdowne Road, Dublin 4, Ireland

© Statistical and Social Inquiry Society of Ireland, 1990

ISBN 1-872002-02-1

Cover illustration: This is the female figure, emblematic of Irish nationhood, painted by Sir John Lavery that was used, in reverse, on the series of bank notes issued in 1928. The figure now features on the watermark of the current Irish note series, issued from 1976 onward.
Portrait reproduced by kind permission of the Central Bank of Ireland.

Cover design and text illustrations by Alanna Corballis
Typeset in 10/11 Bembo by Printset & Design Limited, Dublin
Printed at the Sign of the Three Candles by
Aston Colour Press Limited, Dublin.

CONTENTS

PART III: TOWARDS THE TWENTY-FIRST CENTURY

INTRODUCTION

Currency and banking have a relatively long tradition in Ireland. Coins have circulated for about 1,000 years and banking has been practised for some 300 years. Significant financial change was a feature of earlier periods, as it has been over the past twenty-five years. Looking ahead, financial institutions will continue to experience major changes during the 1990s. Against this background, an appreciation of the past can contribute to an understanding of the present, while influence over future events can be improved by a greater awareness of how changes were accommodated in the past.

With this in mind, a review of the evolution of currency and banking in Ireland, both in the Republic and in Northern Ireland, is presented here, together with a preview of some of the major changes that will be occurring in the decades ahead. The emphasis throughout is on the structural changes that have taken place. A wide range of publications on Irish banking has been drawn upon, many of which are cited in the Bibliography.

The review is divided into three parts. The origins and development of money and banking up to the 1960s are outlined in Part I; the significant changes that occurred in recent decades, including those experienced in the 1980s, are highlighted in Part II; and Part III looks towards the twenty-first century and integration within Europe, with the emphasis on monetary policy and prudential supervision of banks, other financial institutions and the capital markets. Many of the issues raised are relevant to the debate that is currently taking place about the expected changes in the financial sector during the 1990s.

This book was born out of a paper presented to the Statistical and Social Inquiry Society of Ireland at Queen's University, Belfast, on 1 December 1988. The Council of the Society decided that it would be worthwhile to have the paper circulated more widely and arranged for its publication by the Institute of Public Administration. The Society wishes to thank the Institute for editing the material.

It is hoped that the story of banking in Ireland that emerges will be of particular interest to those in banks, building societies, stockbroking, insurance and other financial institutions, and to students of economics, business, banking, finance, accounting, public administration, insurance, law, history and various professional courses with banking as a core subject. It may also be of interest to those concerned with public affairs and to the media.

The author wishes to extend his gratitude to the following individuals: J.J. Sexton, President of the Statistical and Social Inquiry Society of Ireland (1986-89), for his encouragement and support; N.J. Gibson, who proposed the vote of thanks at the 1988 meeting in Belfast; and R.D.C. Black, D. de Buitleir, J. Doherty, M. Casey, P. Charleton, L.M. Cullen, T. O'Connell, C. Ó Gráda and D. Sugrue for their helpful comments on earlier drafts of the manuscript. The author also wishes to thank Angela Whelan for her thorough bibliographical assistance and Rita Flaherty, Carmel Loughlin and Cora McGonigle for bearing competently and patiently with the material through its various drafts. The views expressed are the personal responsibility of the author.

The Statistical and Social Inquiry Society of Ireland
and the publishers wish to thank the
Irish Bankers' Federation
for generous financial support towards the publication
of this book

PART I

THE ORIGINS

COINAGE

Hiberno-Norse coin (c. 1035), with the head of King Sitric, used during Norse occupation of Dublin

With the re-emergence of exchange following the Dark Ages, coins began to be used extensively throughout Europe. They were first issued in Ireland by the Norse Settlement in Dublin during the 990s, many centuries later than in other European countries, including England, Wales and Scotland. In the next two centuries, the acceptance of the use of coinage was relatively slow. The absence of the use of coins in Ireland before this time may reflect the existence over the previous millennium of a relatively highly developed, but localised legal code and counting arrangements that accommodated trading and exchange. With the arrival of the Normans in 1169, issues of Irish coins were made more frequently and this continued for some three centuries, up to around 1500. From then on, however, the minting of coins in Ireland was discouraged by the English monarchy.

The circulation of coins, which was probably centred on the ports and other major towns, existed side by side with barter for at least 700 years until after the emergence of banking-type activities in the 1680s. Thereafter, barter began to recede more rapidly and the currency notes issued by private bankers, which were for uneven amounts, began to form an increasing, but small part of the growing currency circulation. Gold coins, rather than silver, probably played a greater role from 1717 onwards, when Sir Isaac Newton (then master of the mint in England) mistakenly overvalued gold relative to silver by setting the official price of the gold guinea, in terms of silver, at twenty-one shillings.

The design and availability of the coinage from around 1500 up to about 1600 was very unsatisfactory. Irish coins tended to percolate abroad for many reasons — trading, movement of troops, discharge of royal levies, and contributions towards financing wars in which England participated. Outflows of Irish-minted coins tended to be replaced and augmented by 'Irish' coins of a relatively inferior content that were provided from

Coins were minted in Reginald's Tower in Waterford during the 12th and 13th centuries

MONEY OF NECESSITY
Historically, when expenditure by the authorities outstripped their normal capacity to raise revenue, 'money of necessity' was usually created by reducing the value of the existing currency. The metal content of the coinage was reduced (debased) or additional currency notes were printed. James II, for example, helped to finance his campaign in Ireland by using metal from cannons ('gunmoney') to strike new coins. The purchasing power of such money diminished after being put into circulation, since it led to higher prices.

More recently, money of necessity has been put into circulation by printing currency notes and borrowing from central banks.

DEVALUATION OF
CURRENCY
A reduction or depreciation in the value of a country's currency relative to the currencies of other countries.

England to pay for Irish raw materials and the financing of Crown activities, including garrisons, in Ireland. Apart from the minting of 'money of necessity' by the monarchy from time to time, no major Irish mints existed from about 1500, and there were royal prohibitions from the time of Henry VII on transporting to Ireland the more valuable English coins that were intended for circulation in England. Apart from Irish and English coins, there was an appreciable circulation during the sixteenth century of continental coins, especially Spanish, which became more abundant as the century drew to a close, when the Spanish dollar reigned supreme internationally.

Over the next two centuries, from 1600 to 1800, there was an improvement in the condition of the coinage. Despite the royal prohibitions, high-quality English coins found their way into circulation in Ireland, especially after the introduction of the gold guinea in England in 1663. Attractive coins of other European nations — Spanish, Portuguese and French — continued to percolate into circulation. Such developments helped to meet the demands for currency and, in addition, many merchants issued their own tokens in the eighteenth century to facilitate trade.

There are some suggestions that the coins issued in Dublin in the tenth century were similar to those in circulation in other Norse settlements in Europe at that time. We know, however, that as far back as 1200, Irish and English silver coins were interchangeable at par in Ireland and that this situation continued for the next 250 years or so. This was because both sets of coins, though different in design, were similar in size and silver content. In 1460, steps were taken to increase the supply of coinage by devaluing or reducing the silver content of the existing Irish coins. In those days, devaluation was a major technical undertaking: existing coins had to be withdrawn and melted down, then restruck into a larger number of new coins of smaller silver content.

The devaluation of 1460 drove a wedge between

DEBASEMENT OF
COINAGE
*A decline in the value
of coins owing to a
reduction in their metal
content, as a result of
official policy. Debasing
the coinage reduced its
value in much the same
way as devaluation or
pursuit of an
inflationary policy
nowadays reduces the
value of a currency.*

*Henry VIII introduced
the harp to Irish coins
in the 1530s. He was
wont to use the initial
of his wife (on this
groat, A for Anne
Boleyn, H for Henry),
but later he settled for
HR (Henry rex)*

REVALUATION OF
CURRENCY
*A rise or appreciation in
the value of a country's
currency relative to the
currencies of other
countries.*

the Irish and English coins, since they no longer contained a similar amount of silver and, from that time onwards, the Irish currency was independently recognised in the course of commerce and trade. By 1487, the exchange rate had depreciated to one and a half Irish to one English, at which level it seems to have more or less remained until it was depreciated further in the 1550s.

The coinage was debased or devalued on a number of occasions in the 1500s — at the time of the Geraldine Rebellion of 1534-35, in the decade up to 1561, and at the end of Elizabeth's reign. This was done in order to contribute towards defraying the relatively heavy expenses that the English monarchy incurred in Ireland. In other words, devaluation was regarded as a substitute in time of war for collecting taxes and levies. It was during the time of one of these monetary disturbances, probably in the mid-1530s, that Henry VIII formally recognised the Irish pound as a unit of account and introduced the harp coinage into circulation. In 1601, Elizabeth I introduced copper coinage. The minting of coins was made the prerogative of the monarchy and, despite transport costs, was mainly conducted in England, presumably to give the monarchy maximum control over the introduction of new coins into circulation in Ireland. After depreciating in the 1550s, the exchange rate appreciated in 1561 to one and one-third Irish to one English. It remained at around that level for forty years, until the 1601-03 period when there was monetary chaos and a marked depreciation, to close on four Irish to one English, following the defeat of the Irish and Spanish at Kinsale in 1601.

After 1603, the exchange rate appreciated again to much the same level as in the closing decades of the previous century — namely, one and one-third Irish to one English. However, at the time of the Cromwellian Plantation of Ireland in the 1650s, a one-for-one parity seems to have been established. After 1660, this was followed by a depreciation of up to 8 per cent in the Irish exchange rate.

James II paid his army in 'gunmoney' — melted down cannon struck into coins. One measure he took to increase money supply was to restrike half-crowns (top) into crowns (bottom)

Jonathan Swift, satirist of 'those worthy gentlemen, the bankers'

As already mentioned, the coinage that was specifically provided by the monarchy for circulation in Ireland during the seventeenth century was supplemented with a growing mixture of English and continental coins of higher value. The external coins of relatively higher value were retained in Ireland in preference to the relatively low-quality coinage provided from England for circulation in Ireland. Eventually, following the striking of 'gunmoney' by James II (from copper and bronze extracted by melting down cannon, which has left us with the phrase 'not worth a brass farthing'), a reform of the Irish coinage was conducted in 1689. (This was, again, a time of domestic struggle in Ireland, the outcome of which was awaited with much interest by the major powers in Europe.) This monetary reform resulted in the re-establishment of the Irish currency at a fixed rate of exchange of thirteen Irish pence to twelve English pence. This was to prevail without interruption for over a hundred years; it appears to have been based on the silver content of the international mixture of coins circulating in Ireland relative to that of the coins in England. Europe may have been closer to being a single monetary area in those days than in any period since.

The value of the diversified coinage in circulation increased over the eighteenth century, from about £0.5 million in the 1720s to over £1 million some fifty years later. Nevertheless, a distinct shortage of well-designed coins continued to prevail throughout the eighteenth century — a phenomenon also observable in a number of European countries. Despite the need for an adequate supply of currency, a patent issued to a Mr Wood in the 1720s, which would have rapidly increased the circulation of copper coinage in Ireland by about 25 per cent, was withdrawn within two years of being granted. This was because of a campaign waged by Jonathan Swift in *The Drapier's Letters* about the inflationary implications of introducing into circulation what has since been known as Wood's half-pence. No noteworthy

STERLING AREA
A term officially used to
describe the group of
countries that based
their currencies on
sterling. Sterling was
used for making
payments within some
of these countries; in
others, it was relied
upon as an international
monetary reserve, to
which the local currency
was rigidly linked.

LEGAL TENDER
A method of payment
that may be
lawfully offered and
that the creditor is
obliged by law to accept
unconditionally in
respect of the discharge
of a debt. The notes
and coins issued by the
Central Bank of Ireland
are the only forms of
legal tender in the
Republic.

changes in the composition or condition of the coinage were to occur over the eighteenth century other than the increasing inflows of gold coins from England, especially in the 1790s.

Major changes were introduced in Britain in the opening decades of the nineteenth century. The gold sovereign was established by the Coinage Act of 1816 and replaced the guinea, which had been the main gold coin since 1663. Newly designed silver coins, not as valuable as the sovereign, were also introduced into circulation. With the commitment to monetary stability following the currency upheavals of the Napoleonic era, together with the laying of the foundations of the sterling area throughout the British colonies and overseas possessions and the amalgamation of the Irish and British currencies in 1826, the way was now opened for the introduction of the recently designed and reformed British currency into widespread circulation in Ireland. From then onwards, the quality of the coinage was of a high standard and the demand for coins, including sovereigns and half sovereigns, was fully met by an increase in the circulation of British currency in Ireland. Although sovereigns were the only form of legal tender in Ireland in the nineteenth century, the amount in circulation did not keep pace with the growth in bank deposits. Furthermore, as part of the arrangements for financing World War I, sovereigns ceased to be issued by the banks and were replaced mainly by Irish bank notes, which were temporarily extended legal tender status over the period 1914 to 1919. Thus, in the early 1920s the coinage in active circulation consisted solely of British silver and copper coins.

This situation existed until December 1928, when the Irish government launched a distinctive Irish silver and copper coinage, recommended by a committee under the chairmanship of W.B. Yeats, in substitution for the British coins in circulation. Arrangements were also made for the gradual repatriation of British coinage as it was withdrawn from circulation. Some modifications have been

The striking of a coin
in medieval times

made to the metal content of the Irish coinage from time to time and a newly designed Irish coinage was introduced in 1971, when the decimal currency system was adopted. However, it was not until Ireland joined the European Monetary System (EMS) — some fifty years after the Irish coinage was introduced into circulation — that the decisive conditions were created by the break in the fixed link with sterling which led to the virtual disappearance of British currency from circulation in Ireland in the early 1980s. However, almost all the coins in Northern Ireland continue to be British, as has been the situation since 1826. Current indications are that in the Republic the design, size, weight and metal content of the coinage will be modified in the 1990s, with the introduction of a one pound coin and the replacement of the existing coins with a more convenient series.

PRIVATE BANKING: 1700s

PRIVATE BANKS
The first banks to be
established in Ireland
emerged in the period
1680 to 1720; some
survived as independent
institutions up to the
closing decades of the
19th century.
Constituted as private
partnerships, the
partners were limited by
law to six in number
and were fully
responsible for all the
bank's liabilities.

Although Irish banking cannot claim direct links with the Italian banking dynasties of the thirteenth century, it can be traced back to the 1680s, when currency notes were introduced in Ireland alongside the circulation of coins. That was the time when the foundations for the rise in confidence and economic prosperity of the eighteenth century were being laid. Initially, the currency notes took the form of receipts issued by goldsmiths, coin exchangers and merchants located in Dublin and other major ports, who acted as managers and custodians of coins on behalf of their owners or savers. It was the emergence of the practice of making payments by transfer of the goldsmiths' receipts (rather than withdrawing the coins themselves) that conferred the status of money, or medium of exchange, on these receipts and led to their being described as currency notes. The value of such notes in circulation rose from about £0.5 million in the 1720s to around £1 million in the 1750s — a level that was not exceeded again until the 1780s.

Many merchants issued their own coins or tokens in the 18th century to facilitate trade. One side of this goldsmith's token states: 'I promise to pay the bearer two pence, Wm. Ringland, Belfast, 1734'

The essential features of modern banking began to emerge in Ireland from the late seventeenth century onwards. Apart from the custodial features of early banking, it was recognised in the early eighteenth century that the custodians of gold coins and valuables also had the ability to engage in lending. They could lend provided they retained the confidence of those who deposited the gold coins with them. As long as the receipts for the gold deposited continued to circulate for the purposes of effecting payments and were not presented for conversion into gold coins, the custodians of such coins, whether goldsmiths or merchants, could issue receipts made out to the bearer in excess of their coin holdings. Up to a point, the excess issues of receipts helped to maintain the amount of money in circulation, since only a certain proportion of the receipts issued in respect of the deposits of gold circulated freely as money.

As the self-confidence of the goldsmiths and merchants grew and their lending began to exceed their holdings of gold coins, they became engaged in creating credit, that is, adding to the overall supply of means of payments or money in circulation as a result of granting credit to borrowers. The evolution of this practice helped to finance investment and maintain the level of spending. However, it also exposed the economy and society to the risks of excessive credit creation and the collapse of banking institutions. The collapse of a bank could easily arise as a result of the rapid conversion of currency notes into gold coins that outstretched the capacity of the bank to continue converting its assets into gold coins. The failure of a bank could also arise as a result of imprudent lending that could not be recovered, thereby resulting in the writing off of the bank's capital and the erosion of its capacity to repay its deposits in full.

During the period 1700 to 1750, Irish banking was highly innovative by the international standards of the time, which were being set in Scotland. This was the era when private banking flourished and

JOINT STOCK BANKS
The name given to
those large banks
established in the 1820s
and 1830s by means of
the issue of stock or
shares to a large number
of stock- or shareholders.
(Today, such banks are
known as clearing
banks.) Shareholders
were responsible for the
full amount of the
bank's liabilities: the
principle of limited
liability was not
extended to bank
shareholders until 1879.

LIQUIDITY
A quality possessed by
assets that can be
readily turned into cash
at little cost. Also
known as 'liquid assets'.
Such assets can be
'domestic' or 'foreign',
depending on where
they are located. A
market for an asset is
regarded as being liquid
if the asset can be sold
quickly and close to its
current market value.

it was not until the early decades of the next century that private joint stock banks, the forerunners of the present-day clearing banks, emerged. By 1750, there were banks in some eight centres throughout Ireland whose main business followed this pattern: banks provided credit to merchants by issuing currency notes, which enabled them to purchase items such as grain from farmers, especially for export. Subsequently, the farmers used the notes to pay their rents to the landlords. Then the landlords exchanged the notes for the foreign proceeds of the exports that had been lodged by the merchants to discharge their original borrowings from the banks. The landlords then used the foreign currency to pay for imports and to finance consumption and investment abroad. Seasonal requirements, therefore, had a significant influence on the business of banking in Ireland down the centuries until recent decades.

Banking in Ireland in the eighteenth century was associated to a significant extent with the interests of the landed aristocracy, unlike in other western European countries where it was based primarily on the needs of the emerging merchant classes and of the state. The Irish banks were primarily concerned with facilitating the transfer of agricultural output from the countryside to Dublin and abroad, and placing the proceeds of the sale of that output at the disposal of the landlords. However, around mid-century, a number of banks that had actively engaged in supporting the growing needs of the merchant classes collapsed in the wake of disappointing economic circumstances, strained liquidity conditions and accompanying bad debt experiences.

This situation gave rise to legislation in 1756 that excluded merchants involved in foreign trade from engaging in the business of banking. As a result, a division between banking and commerce was instituted (which, even today, is carefully guarded in developed countries) and led to a strengthening of the influence of the landed gentry. Consequently, private banking in the second half of the eighteenth

This beautiful coin, dating from the 1670s, may have been issued by Dublin Corporation. It shows St Patrick banishing the snakes on one side and King David playing the harp on the other

century failed to display the highly innovative character of its earlier years, despite more favourable economic circumstances, and did not keep abreast of developments in Scottish banking. The last expansionary, but short-lived phase of private banking in Ireland occurred during the Napoleonic wars.

Irish banking was not well prepared for adapting itself to the economic depression following the 1798 rebellion in Ireland and the Napoleonic wars on the continent. It relied too much on land as security, lacked a dynamic commercial influence and was overstretched following the exceptionally large increases in currency during the war years. Consequently, some private banks failed again between the closing years of the 1790s and the early 1820s; by the 1890s, all the private banks that had survived were integrated with the joint stock banks, established from 1824 onwards.

The savings bank movement, which had its origins in Scotland, was launched in Ireland around 1815, when the first savings bank was started in the parish of Stillorgan, Co. Dublin. By 1820, all of the trustee savings banks now in operation throughout Ireland had been established. Furthermore, within a few years, an important phase in the development of Irish banking was to begin, with the establishment of reasonably widely owned joint stock banks with unlimited shareholder liability.

With the introduction of joint stock banking, a firm foundation was set in a remarkably short number of years — between 1824 and 1836 — for the existing clearing bank system. This was achieved despite a short-lived, but serious run on existing banks in 1836 in connection with declining confidence in the adventurous Agricultural and Commercial Bank of Ireland. This joint stock bank, which opened its first branch in Nenagh, Co. Tipperary, in 1834, collapsed without loss to its noteholders and depositors but at the expense of its shareholders. It failed because of a lack of planning and foresight by the promoters, shareholders of limited means, unsuitable management and staff, misappropriation of funds and reckless lending and record-keeping that did not keep track of the amount of currency notes put into circulation, mainly on a commission basis.

CENTRAL BANKING: FIRST STEPS

Most national or central banks were established or evolved because of the financial needs of the state, especially in time of war. The first bank of this type that eventually became a central bank was established in Sweden in 1668. In England, what is nowadays known as a central bank came into being when the Bank of England was established in 1694. There was a similar intent in Scotland when the Bank of Scotland was established in 1695. However, an initiative by the main merchants of Dublin in 1695 to establish 'a public bank or a fund of credit for the encouragement of trade, and supply of the present want of money' faltered. There was no enthusiasm for such a development in Ireland in the late 1690s and early 1700s owing to concern about what was felt to be the excessive influence of the English monarchy on Irish affairs. Neither was there a crisis in the public finances or serious instability in the banking system — the two main reasons for the emergence of central banks.

The lack of enthusiasm in Ireland for extending power and privileges over financial matters to the monarchy was partly fostered by Jonathan Swift — who did not hold bankers in high esteem — in *The Drapier's Letters*. However, in 1721, a charter for a national bank similar to the Bank of England was granted, subject to approval by Irish parliamentarians. Because of the absence of political support and also because of mistrust in the 1720s of all financial innovation after the South Sea Bubble, the charter did not receive the support of Irish politicians. Consequently, the emergence of national banking was postponed for over sixty years. In the intervening period, the Irish

SOUTH SEA BUBBLE
Popular name for the first major stock market boom in Europe, which occurred in 1718-20. Exotic images of trading with the East led to feverish speculation, in London, Amsterdam and Paris, in the shares of a British company. Over-extended investors stampeded to sell South Sea shares, which led to a rapid fall in their price and to the bankruptcy of many who had borrowed heavily to acquire them.

philosopher and economist George Berkeley contributed to keeping the issue alive by making a case for a national bank for Ireland in *The Querist,* published in 1735.

Conditions changed, however, in the second half of the eighteenth century in favour of promoting a national bank. This was partly as a result of the adverse private banking experiences around the mid-century. More important was the indirect impact on the Irish economy and public finances of the international economic disturbances associated with the American War of Independence. Against this background, the deficits in the Irish public finances, which had persisted from the early 1760s, become more pronounced in the late 1770s and early 1780s, leading to relatively substantial increases in borrowings by the Irish Exchequer. This gave a major stimulus to the re-opening of the case for a national bank.

These financial developments, together with the spirit of independence kindled in Ireland through contact with France and the rest of continental Europe but particularly in the light of the American Declaration of Independence in 1776, generated the political support which was previously lacking for the services of a national bank. The first faltering steps were taken towards promoting what is nowadays regarded as a central bank when, in 1783, the Bank of Ireland (now a clearing bank) was established by the Irish Parliament. It was given a virtual monopoly of the right to issue bank notes throughout the country.

EXCHEQUER ACCOUNT
The principal bank account of the government, which is nowadays maintained at the Central Bank. All tax receipts are lodged to this account and government cheques and payment orders are drawn on it.

The management of the Exchequer Account together with the registers of government stocks were entrusted to the Bank of Ireland. In turn, the bank advanced most of the proceeds of its newly issued capital to the Irish Exchequer which, within a decade or so, also extended its borrowings to England in the aftermath of the declaration of war on France by England in 1793. There was a ceiling of 5 per cent on the rate of interest that the Bank of Ireland could apply to lending.

For the next forty years or so, the Bank of Ireland

GOLD STANDARD
The name of the
international monetary
system that prevailed in
the 19th century and up
to the 1930s. At that
time, countries fixed
their currencies to a
specific quantity of gold
which could be
transferred freely
between them. This
resulted in fixed rates of
exchange between
currencies, which could
be exchanged for gold.
International cooperation
was required to allow
gold to be moved
between countries and to
discourage them from
taking domestic policy
measures to offset the
effects of inflows and
outflows of gold on their
banks and local interest
rates.

LENDER OF LAST RESORT
The public institution
(i.e. the Central Bank)
that stands ready in
normal circumstances, as
well as in a financial
crisis, to lend to solvent
banks which need cash
or transferable funds
immediately.

was the dominant influence in the banking system, even though it had no branches outside Dublin until the mid-1820s. It was not exposed to serious competition and accounted for a major share of the note issue, especially in the decade 1815 to 1825, since it was the only large bank (that is, with more than six shareholders) that was permitted to issue notes throughout the country. However, the Bank of Ireland was not destined to evolve into what is nowadays known as a central bank, although it continued to develop decisively in this direction up to about 1850.

With the transfer of the seat of government from Dublin to London following the coming into effect of the Act of Union on 1 January 1801, the management of the financing of the state shifted from Dublin to London. This limited the role that the Bank of Ireland could play in the early decades of the nineteenth century, especially in the period following the amalgamation of the British and Irish Exchequers and Public Debts in 1817. Further constraints were placed on the Bank of Ireland in the second half of the last century with the passage of the Bankers' (Ireland) Act 1845, with the emergence of the international gold standard and the establishment of the Bank of England as the lender of last resort for the whole of the sterling area, including Ireland.

Up to the middle of the nineteenth century, the Bank of Ireland acted in a limited way as a bankers' bank and as a hesitant lender of last resort, although it provided in central bank-like fashion strong leadership in establishing currency note and cheque clearings arrangements between the banks. When joint stock banking was on the horizon, in the early 1820s, the Bank of Ireland pressed hard to preserve its dominant position, especially in relation to the issue of currency notes which, after 1821, was confined to a radius of sixty-five miles from Dublin. It was reluctant to accept the emergence of joint stock banks, although it did compete directly with them throughout the country particularly from the mid-1820s onwards. When the 1845 Bankers' Act

A £1 note issued in
1825 by the Cork office
of the Provincial Bank
of Ireland, one of seven
joint stock banks
founded between 1824
and 1836

PRIVATE BANK NOTES
These were the currency
notes or paper money
introduced into
circulation from the
1680s onwards by the
private and, later, the
joint stock and clearing
banks. Their issue was
prohibited in 1929,
after the introduction of
official notes and coins
with legal tender status.
Currency notes continue
to be issued by banks in
Northern Ireland.

was passed, the remaining privileges of the Bank
of Ireland in relation to the issue of notes in the
Dublin region were removed by allowing the note-
issuing joint stock banks in existence at that time
to issue their notes in the Dublin region. All note-
issuing banks could issue their notes freely
throughout the country after 1845.

The 1845 legislation provided for more effective
competition between banks. It was also designed
to discourage increases in the circulation of private
bank notes from displacing gold and silver and
eventually Bank of England notes from circulation.
A domestic policy of substituting the note issue of
the Bank of England for that of the other banks was
being firmly implemented in Britain in the
mid-1840s. It had also been an objective of British
foreign policy since the 1820s to promote, directly
or indirectly, the circulation of British currency
throughout the British Empire. Against this
background, the emergence in Ireland in the 1840s
of an institution similar to the Bank of England,
with a monopoly of the note issue, was probably
not being encouraged. Nevertheless, it is of interest
to recall that some forty years later the Chancellor

of the Exchequer reminded the Bank of Ireland of its special position among banks in Ireland at the height of the Munster Bank crisis in 1885. At the time of the 1845 legislation, the Bank of Ireland was given the sole right of handling the government's cash operations; in addition, the ceiling on the rate of interest it could charge on loans was abolished.

These legislative changes placed all banks on a more or less equal footing and created conditions that enabled the Bank of Ireland to concentrate to a greater extent than before on commercial banking. A further boost to the Bank of Ireland's commercial role occurred in 1855 when it sanctioned the use of overdrafts, and in 1864 when it commenced paying interest on deposits and was granted the power to extend credit, secured by mortgage. The increasing competitiveness of the Bank of Ireland probably encouraged its competitors to rely less on it for temporary support or accommodation. From the 1860s onwards, similar services were readily available in London to the other banks from institutions that they did not regard as major direct competitors, thus weakening the leadership of the Bank of Ireland.

By the time independence was re-established in the 1920s, the Bank of Ireland had developed primarily along commercial lines and was not destined to evolve towards central banking in the recently established state. A serious conflict of interest would have arisen if the primary functions of a central bank were to be vested in a competitive profit-oriented bank that was part of the private sector, as international experience with the evolution of central banking in the nineteenth century had clearly demonstrated. There was also increasing international recognition in the 1920s, following the establishment of the Federal Reserve System in the USA just before World War I and the inflationary experiences in Europe after the war, of the desirability of maintaining central banking independent of the authorities.

These international concerns received support in Ireland in the 1920s through the reluctance of the existing banks to become closely associated with extending financial support to the newly established authorities in Ireland. At the same time, however, the banks were not enthusiastic about losing their right to issue currency notes to an embryonic central bank. Indeed, it could be said that the banks were not receptive to the idea of establishing a central bank — a point of view that was expressed on a number of occasions up to the early 1940s. This echoed the resistance of commercial banks in other countries during the nineteenth century to central banks' acquiring a monopoly of the note issue and extending their influence over the banking system. It was against this conservative background in monetary matters that the forerunner of the Central Bank of Ireland, namely the Currency Commission, was established in 1927 and central banking evolved in subsequent decades.

Giving change of a halfpenny (top) or a quarterpenny in the 13th century often entailed cutting through the soft metal with a knife between the double lines of the cross. These coins date from the time of Henry III (1216-72)

MONETARY INSTABILITY: EARLY EXPERIENCES

The wars in Europe between 1793 and 1815 and the implementation of the Act of Union had significant implications for deficits in the public finances, banking, the currency and the exchange rate. After the British declaration of war on France in 1793, the Bank of Ireland became engaged in financing part of the large increase in military expenditure which was outstripping revenue receipts. Within a decade or so of being established, the Bank of Ireland was also engaging in relatively large increases in lending and issues of bank notes to the private sector. Military spending increased substantially after 1794 and led to a significant increase in the public debt over the twenty-year period 1795 to 1815.

In the decade 1794 to 1804, there was a five-fold increase in the amount of Bank of Ireland notes in circulation — from £0.5 million in 1794 to some £2.5 million in 1804. Most of this increase occurred between 1798 and 1803, when the Irish pound was floating against sterling, gold and, of course, the continental currencies that remained tied to gold. Both the long-established and recently launched private banks (of which there were over forty in operation outside Dublin in 1804) were also engaging in relatively large issues of currency notes during the closing years of the eighteenth century and the opening years of the nineteenth; their note circulation peaked at a level of some £1.3 million around 1803, compared with around £1 million in the 1780s. However, the contribution of the private banks to the overall increase in the note circulation between 1798 and 1803 was overshadowed by that of the Bank of Ireland.

Along with such large increases in note circulation, there was also evidence of a change in the relationship between exports and imports. In the first year of each decade of the eighteenth century, there is evidence that exports exceeded imports. But in the first year of each of the first two decades of the nineteenth century, an excess of imports over exports is recorded, despite the opportunities to increase Irish exports and the unavailability of certain imports in war-time conditions.

The relatively large increases in the currency issue after 1793 together with a fall in the exchange rate between 1797 and 1804, led to the appointment in 1804 of what may be regarded as the first-ever official committee of inquiry — the Irish Currency Committee — into the relationship between credit creation, currency issues, prices, external payments and the exchange rate in a small open economy. However, little attention was given by the committee to the monetary and exchange rate implications of the relatively large fiscal deficits that were being incurred to finance military expenditure nor, indeed, did the committee consider the exchange rate implications of the real or non-monetary distortions arising from the hostilities.

It was not surprising, therefore, following the floating in 1797 of both the Irish pound and sterling against gold and the relatively large increase in the Irish currency circulation, that the Irish pound

This Fenian Bond for $20, issued on 17 February 1866, was one of many such bonds sold in the USA from 1862 to 1867 to support the cause of Irish independence. This bond bears the signature of 'John O'Mahony, Agent for the Irish Republic', a prominent member of the Fenian movement. Many banks honoured these bonds at a later date

experienced sharp fluctuations vis-à-vis sterling which was also floating against all other currencies, including the continental currencies that continued to be underpinned by gold. The Irish pound devalued against sterling by some 10 per cent between 1797 and 1804, then appreciated up to 1813 and subsequently devalued sharply, so that by 1815 it had reverted to much the same level as in 1804. The floating exchange rate arrangements continued until 1821, when both sterling and the Irish pound were again fixed to gold at the same relationship of thirteen Irish pounds to twelve pounds sterling that had prevailed in 1797.

This consolidated the 10 per cent appreciation of the Irish pound against sterling that occurred between 1815 and 1821. It is appropriate to recall that it was during 1817 that the Irish Exchequer and Public Debt were effectively integrated with the British Exchequer and Public Debt. This fiscal development may have made a contribution to the re-establishment of the exchange rate against sterling at its 1797 level and to diverting attention from the implications of the outstanding external debt vis-à-vis Britain, which had continued to increase between 1798 and 1815.

BANK LIQUIDITY
The cash and other short-term encashable assets held by a bank to meet over-the-counter withdrawals of funds and adverse cheque clearings vis-à-vis other banks. An adequate level of liquidity, or liquid assets (both foreign and domestic), promotes confidence in a bank and supports it in conducting its business from day to day and in realising its corporate targets. The liquid assets expressed in foreign currencies are referred to as 'external liquidity', while those expressed in Irish pounds are called 'domestic liquidity'.

After the Battle of Waterloo in 1815, there was a period of severe economic contraction and falling prices in Ireland, which contrasted with the improvement in economic conditions and inflation that prevailed between 1793 and 1815. Three factors contributed to this economic depression, although the extent to which each did so is not clear. Firstly, there was the indirect impact of the international depression following the peace settlement at the Congress of Vienna in 1815. Second, there were the spillover effects of the pursuit of the singularly British monetary objective of restoring the pre-war value of money by resuming the conversion of Bank of England notes into gold at the rate that prevailed in 1797, even though prices had risen substantially in the meantime. And lastly, there was the direct locally created effects of the relatively tighter monetary conditions that seem to have been applied in Ireland.

It may be the case that the monetary restraint in Ireland was pursued with a view to preparing the way for the return to the fixed level of the exchange rate between the Irish pound and sterling that prevailed throughout the eighteenth century. It may also have been pursued to achieve the narrower banking objective of building up bank liquidity in anticipation of the possible presentation of outstanding bank notes that might follow the amalgamation of the Irish pound and sterling at parity. It is noteworthy, in the context of the objectives of British foreign policy, that the currencies were amalgamated on a one-for-one basis in 1826, just five years after the reintroduction of the fixed exchange rate. Apart from the thirteenth and early fourteenth century custom of exchanging Irish and English coins on a one-for-one basis, this was the second occasion that the currencies were deliberately united. (The first occurred under Cromwell in the 1650s and seems to have lasted for less than a decade.)

British currency circulated freely throughout Ireland until 1928 — seven years after political independence — when the Irish pound was

ONE-FOR-ONE,
NO-MARGINS BASIS
When the Irish pound was linked to sterling, it exchanged on a one-for-one, no-margins basis with sterling, without payment of any foreign exchange commission or other transaction charges. This occurred because there was no foreign exchange market between these two currencies before 1979. Irrevocable rates of exchange between the European currencies could lead to similar arrangements emerging in Europe as the foreign exchange markets between European currencies become defunct.

introduced into circulation. The reinstated Irish pound was placed on a one-for-one, no-margins basis with sterling for the purposes of maximising confidence in it and avoiding any change in monetary conditions from what would have prevailed if sterling had continued to be the principal currency in circulation. This relationship between the Irish pound and sterling continued for over fifty years, until 1979, when the EMS came into operation and the link with sterling was again broken. However, the two currencies are destined to be amalgamated once more, along with all the other European currencies, on the next occasion — when monetary union in Europe eventually becomes a reality.

MONETARY INTEGRATION WITH THE STERLING AREA

Ireland had been on a *de facto* gold standard since 1717, except during the period of the first modern international monetary crisis — the global monetary upheaval associated with the Napoleonic wars. In 1821, Ireland was integrated into the British gold standard, which recently had been placed on a legal footing as part of the monetary reforms following the restoration of peace in 1815. Within fifty years, London had evolved to become the hub of the international monetary system — a position which it retained until 1914. During the last century, the pace of economic development in the major economies did not lead to serious external imbalances or major confrontations.

The breakdown of the international gold standard followed in the wake of World War I and, from the 1920s, the US dollar and New York were at the centre of the international financial system. Following the acceptance of the gold standard in the 1820s, which minimised the discretionary role of the authorities in monetary affairs, the appropriateness of the gold standard arrangements was not seriously questioned until Keynes expressed serious reservations in 1925 about Churchill's policy of revaluing sterling and winding back prices to the level they were at in 1914. Subsequently, sterling was devalued on a number of occasions — in 1931, 1939, 1949, 1967 and again during the period 1972 to 1976. During these major changes in international monetary arrangements, Ireland continued to remain a member of the sterling area, until it disintegrated after the devaluation of sterling in 1967, and to be linked directly with sterling itself until the EMS came into operation in 1979.

With these rigid exchange rate connections, it is probable that the magnitude of the increases and decreases in prices and interest rates in Ireland over the centuries were similar to those experienced in Britain (excluding the twenty-five year period 1797 to 1821 when movements in prices and interest rates in Ireland may have been more pronounced than in Britain). It is also probable that, apart from short lags, the upward and downward movements in prices and interest rates occurred in both economies around the same time.

Relative stability in prices and interest rates (that is, relative to those in Britain rather than absolute price and interest rate stability) was the result of being on the gold standard and a member of the sterling area. Thus, the growth in the currency circulation in Ireland was directly influenced by the fluctuations in prices and interest rates in Britain. Moreover, it reflected the speed with which barter disappeared in Ireland and the rate at which the Irish economy developed. Since this did not grow as rapidly as the British economy, it is probable that the rate of growth of money in circulation in Ireland, and indeed the rate of expansion of the banking system, was much slower than in Britain (even if the substantial contribution of non-resident balances to the growth of the British banking system were excluded).

The increase over time in the amount of money in circulation and in bank deposits was sustained by the impact of certain developments between

Ireland and abroad. The net result of the money transactions between Ireland and the British Exchequer, plus the excess of domestic receipts from abroad* over domestic payments abroad**, provided the external base for the growth over the centuries in the amount of currency in circulation. It also provided the base for the rise in bank deposits, including those with the savings banks. The net receipts arising from all non-bank transactions with abroad were unavoidably associated with the rise in holdings of external currency (including sovereigns, other foreign coins and British currency notes) and with the accumulation by the banking system of external assets in London.

While the growth in bank deposits was directly associated with the accumulation of external assets abroad by the banks, it was also the case that the growth in bank deposits reflected the increase in the banks' domestic lending. In other words, the accumulation of bank deposits reflected the rise in both the external assets of the banks as well as their domestic lending. However, the rise in the currency circulation was mainly associated with net receipts from abroad, which did not become part of the external assets in London of the banks.

The decreases that occurred from time to time in the level of the currency circulation and in bank deposits were associated with temporary deteriorations in the value of exports (arising from contractions in external markets, bad domestic harvests and adverse movements in the international prices of agricultural products). Such developments also tended to be associated with reductions in the banks' external assets as well as in their domestic lending, the contractions in lending being more

---

* in respect of exports of goods and services, external borrowing and repatriation of foreign assets by residents (other than banks).
** arising from imports of goods and services, repayment of external capital and the acquisition of assets abroad by residents (other than banks).

pronounced when harvests were bad. Outflows of deposits for investment abroad also led to a contraction in the banks' external assets. However, reductions in currency holdings, especially after 1845, would not have led to a corresponding decline in the banks' externally held assets, since most of the currency in circulation was an external asset or the equivalent thereof. Excessive domestic bank lending, contributing to increased imports, capital outflows and a reduction in the banks' external assets, has been much more a feature of the second half of the twentieth century than of earlier times, especially when the period of the Napoleonic wars is excluded.

As the Irish economy was part of the sterling area, one would expect that banks in Ireland were constrained from paying much less for deposits or charging significantly more for credit than the banks in internationally competitive Britain. Moreover, even with banks channelling part of the domestic savings into external assets in the form of balances in London, one would expect also that it did not result in large profitable investment opportunities in Ireland being neglected; the banks had an incentive in the form of expected higher profits to lend in Ireland if the returns were as high or higher than abroad. Furthermore, since major borrowers in Ireland could have direct resort to the financial institutions in London and since profitable investment opportunities in Ireland were always free to attract the externally oriented British investors, one would expect that potentially profitable investment opportunities in Ireland would not be neglected. Irish firms also had the opportunity to raise funds on the Dublin, Cork and Belfast stock exchanges which they had resort to, especially in the period 1870 to 1900 when many Irish businesses became incorporated under the company legislation and raised capital by share issues to the public.

The main reason for the accumulation of external assets by the banks was the emergence, in a free trade environment, of external trade surpluses by the agricultural sector at a time of limited profitable investment opportunities in the rest of the economy and the absence of locally oriented fiscal and regional policies. Conservative domestic attitudes towards investing in Ireland may also have contributed to the relatively large increases in non-bank holdings of British government securities that accompanied significant increases in the banks' external assets.

Taking a broader view, it would be difficult to conclude that economic development in Ireland was held back by the banking system, especially when the experiences of banking with industrial development in the north-eastern part of the economy are taken into consideration. However, what seems surprising, in the context of no exchange rate worries and full membership of the sterling area, was the extent to which the banks held external assets in liquid form rather than diversifying to a greater extent into lending in Britain with a view to enhancing their profits. It seems reasonable to suggest that the accumulation of external liquid assets by the banks did not give rise to a lower level of investment in Ireland when one also considers the extent to which bank credit for seasonal and stock-carrying purposes was provided and that a hard core of overdraft accommodation remained continuously outstanding in support of capital investments.

It should not be concluded that membership of the sterling area did not have a significant impact on the development of the Irish economy. While it is difficult to establish that monetary integration itself impeded economic development, an evaluation of the overall economic effects of integration within the sterling area would have to take into consideration the effects of the budgetary, trade and other economic policies pursued. An historical review that focused specifically on the economic as well as on the monetary features of the union that existed between the Irish and British economies might contribute to forming a deeper appreciation of the economic and monetary implications for Ireland of full integration within the European Community.

JOINT STOCK BANKING:
EARLY DECADES

Branch banking did not emerge until the mid-1820s. This may have been partly associated with the rise in commercial activity being centred initially on the larger towns rather than being more widespread throughout the country. Following the increase in familiarity with currency notes during the Napoleonic wars, the reduction in the number of private banks outside Dublin to about ten and the improvement in the economic situation following the severely depressed conditions of the early 1820s, a more widespread and growing demand for the services of banks began to occur. This demand was supported by a number of legislative changes in the 1820s. Only one major bank existed in the early 1820s, the Bank of Ireland, which was located in Dublin and had not yet embarked on establishing branches throughout the country. Thus, an opportunity existed for joint stock banking to emerge, as was occurring abroad especially in Scotland but also in England.

The distinctive feature of joint stock banks was their large number of reasonably widely dispersed wealthy shareholders with unlimited liability. Bank customers, therefore, developed a high degree of confidence in joint stock banks. This was in marked contrast to their attitude towards single-branch private banks in earlier times, which relied excessively for their supporting capital on the fortunes of a small number of individuals or families (by law, no more than six). The circumstances were now propitious for the spread of branch banking and joint stock banking readily lent itself to this on account of the confidence it generated with prospective depositors and holders of bank notes throughout the country.

The need to open up entry into banking and to provide competitive banking services throughout the country was recognised by the authorities following strong representations from business interests in Belfast. Indeed, the authorities probably

CLEARING BANKS
Banks that specialise in retail or individual consumer banking, providing their customers, particularly personal customers, with current account facilities. Such banks also have arrangements between themselves for exchanging one another's cheques and settling their net differences by transferring balances held at the Central Bank. Irish clearing banks have also diversified into other areas of business — corporate, wholesale and international banking.

In Ireland, clearing banks are also known as 'associated banks' (because of legislative provisions that associated them for certain purposes with the Central Bank when it was being established), as well as commercial or retail banks.

recognised that, apart from the Bank of Ireland which was concentrating on Dublin, there would be little opposition from established bankers to legislative measures that would open up the way for joint stock banking throughout the country. Legislative changes in the early 1820s made provision for joint stock banks that wished to issue currency notes outside a radius of sixty-five miles from Dublin, in direct competition with the Bank of Ireland. Such banks would also be free to establish themselves within the Dublin region, provided they refrained from issuing currency notes, thereby leaving the Bank of Ireland with the sole right of note issue in the Dublin area.

The most significant development in Irish banking in the last century, and indeed up to the 1960s, was the establishment of seven successful joint stock banks over the twelve-year period 1824 to 1836. Apart from the Bank of Ireland (which was already established by charter some forty years earlier) and the Munster and Leinster Bank Limited (which emerged some fifty years later in the southern region of the country), all of the other clearing banks operating in Ireland up to the 1960s were established in the twelve hectic years up to 1836. The emerging banks in this period fall into three groupings: three Presbyterian-supported banks centred on Belfast; two in the Dublin region with some external capital backing to compete with the Bank of Ireland (except in regard to the issue of notes); and two, with significant backing of external capital and with head offices in London, which concentrated on the rest of Leinster, Munster and Connacht but not to the exclusion of Ulster.

The first joint stock bank — the Northern Banking Company — was founded in 1824 in Belfast. The northern region of the country did not have a strong private banking tradition. By the early decades of the nineteenth century, this part of the country was becoming a major centre of economic growth and developing a strong demand for banking facilities, rather than continuing to rely on coinage, especially gold. It was in response to this need that the Northern Banking Company was established by a group of local shareholders with an industrial background. In the Dublin region the Hibernian Bank, with Catholic support, was established in 1825, thereby challenging the monopoly of the Bank of Ireland there. The Provincial Bank of Ireland was also established in 1825, with strong Scottish backing and its head office in London. This bank played a major role in promoting competition in Irish banking before a much less competitive banking environment was gradually created over the period 1886 to 1921 through common agreements on a number of issues among the banks themselves.

In 1827, the Belfast Banking Company was established and, in the process, absorbed the two remaining private banks that operated in the north of the country. After a lag of seven years, the National Bank was founded in 1834 by Daniel O'Connell, with sizeable external backing. An objective of this bank was to introduce banking more deeply into the rural communities than was being done by either the Scottish-supported Provincial Bank or the Dublin-oriented, Anglican-supported Bank of Ireland. Only a few years earlier, in 1829, O'Connell, for political purposes, was advocating that bank customers convert their currency notes into gold — that is, he was promoting runs on the banks. The National Bank also established a significant presence in England, both among the larger Irish communities as well as in the City where its head office was located; it was admitted to the prestigious London Clearing Banks Committee in the 1850s.

Daniel O'Connell founded the National Bank of Ireland in 1834, with its head office in London. His objective was to provide banking facilities for the largely Catholic, rural communities in Ireland

The Royal Bank of Ireland, with the support of the Quaker community, was established in 1836 and created a more competitive banking climate within the Dublin region. Later that year, the youngest of the joint stock banks — the Ulster Bank — was established with its head office in Belfast. One of its objectives was to compete primarily in the northern part of the country with the two north-eastern oriented banks that had already been in existence for about a decade and with the Bank of Ireland and the Provincial Bank which were also establishing themselves in Ulster.

The Ulster Bank moved outside the province of Ulster in 1860 when it opened a branch in Sligo; in 1862, it opened a branch in Dublin — the first of the northern-based banks to do so in the capital city. A quarter of a century was to pass before the Northern Banking Company opened a branch in Dublin in 1888, to be followed by the Belfast Banking Company in 1891. (However, the latter was the first northern-based bank to move outside the province of Ulster, in 1850.)

Thus, by 1836 there were just over 130 bank branches located throughout Ireland, compared with no more than a few branches a decade earlier. The introduction of branches to the towns helped to diversify risk for the owners of banks. But they did not extend their banking services to any significant extent to the middle and lower-income groups in rural and urban areas; this only happened in recent times. Indeed, for many decades after their establishment, individual banks were closely identified with a particular religious persuasion (whether Anglican, Presbyterian, Catholic or Quaker) and the wealth and income-earning capacity (whether landed, merchant or professional) of their founders, shareholders and large customers. However, with the passage of time, a growing proportion of the economically active population became involved with banking and this was reflected in the decline of the Protestant proportion of bank officials in the Republic to around 50 per cent in the mid-1930s (Foster, 1988).

In 1836, bank notes in circulation amounted to around £5 million, while deposits with banks were somewhat less, perhaps £4 million. A further boost to competition in the eastern region was given in 1845, when all of the note-issuing joint stock banks in existence at that time were given the right to issue their own notes throughout the whole of the country. Notes outstanding beyond the aggregate level of £6.4 million had to be backed by gold or silver, thereby favouring the growth of bank deposits and the circulation of British currency (that is, sovereigns and Bank of England notes rather than Irish bank notes). By 1845, deposits in the Irish banks had increased to some £8 million.

These developments in joint stock banking were accompanied by a rapid, but short-lived growth in the number of savings banks throughout the country. These numbered seventy-nine in 1836, with aggregate deposits of £1.8 million. Following this rapid rate of increase, many savings banks experienced difficulties, especially during the 1840s, despite the dedication and voluntary support of those associated with the savings bank movement. Confidence was shaken in the mid-1840s when the liability of trustees and managers to make good deficiencies in the funds of a savings bank was removed by the 1844 Savings Bank Act. Another factor that contributed to reducing confidence was the closure of some twenty-five savings banks during the late 1840s. In 1848, three savings banks (the Tralee, Killarney and Cuffe Street bank in Dublin) collapsed at the expense of depositors because of serious frauds.

A Select Committee of Parliament was appointed to inquire into these frauds. As a result, legislation was passed in 1848 which increased the responsibilities of trustees to depositors and provided for the appointment of auditors. This legislation probably did much to prevent a major collapse of the savings bank movement in Ireland. By 1845, aggregate deposits in the savings banks amounted to nearly £3 million. Even in 1914 they did not exceed this level, by which time the number of savings banks in Ireland had gradually fallen to eight through closures and mergers. The savings banks were not direct competitors of the joint stock banks, since the former concentrated their activities among the non-Catholic, lower-income groups especially in larger towns, thereby confining themselves to a relatively small market, particularly outside Ulster.

The experiences of private banking, of the early

savings bank movement and of a number of the small joint stock banks that did not survive highlight the importance of holding an adequate amount of cash and short-term assets, and of continuity in the availability of adequate capital to support a bank's deposit liabilities. Historical experience also shows the need for the application of high standards in respect of probity, competence and capacity. Reliance on the personal wealth of a small number of individuals is not normally conducive to sustaining adequate capital, especially in a bank or other deposit-taking financial institution that wishes to grow in a stable manner.

BANKING STRUCTURE: 1840s ONWARDS

The Munster and Leinster Bank came into existence in 1885, with its head office in Cork. Apart from it, few other joint stock banks of significance were launched or survived after 1836. South Tipperary was the main inland region with a firmly based banking tradition going back to the private banking days of the mid-eighteenth century. In the 1830s three banks, all short-lived, were established in the county, in the prosperous Suir valley with its Quaker settlements. These were the Clonmel National and the Carrick-on-Suir National, both of which were founded in 1836 and merged with the National Bank in 1856, and the Tipperary Joint Stock Bank (better known as Sadleir's Bank), founded in 1838 and which failed in 1856 because of fraud. Its demise resulted in much suffering for many families of modest means, as well as temporary runs on local bank branches.

Although the private joint stock banks became incorporated entities between 1865 and 1869, their shareholders could not avail themselves of the protection of limited liability until legislation was passed in 1879. By 1883, all the banks had extended limited liability to their shareholders, except the Bank of Ireland which did not do so until 1935.

LIMITED LIABILITY
A provision of company law, whereby the liability of the shareholders or owners for a company's debts cannot exceed the capital subscribed plus guarantees entered into by the shareholders or owners.

Bank officials standing outside the Carrick-on-Suir branch of the Bank of Ireland in the late 19th century. The Bank of Ireland, founded in 1783, did not begin to establish branches outside Dublin until the mid-1820s

Prior to the 1880s, it was relatively easy to attract capital into banking, even with unlimited liability. However, it became less easy to do so as a result of the large losses experienced by bank shareholders when the City of Glasgow Bank closed its doors in 1878. Thus, the adoption of the provisions of the 1879 Act encouraged bank shareholders to provide additional capital for banks from the early 1880s onwards. Banks also began to publish their annual accounts on a regular basis in the 1880s. This helped to keep both shareholders and depositors informed from year to year about the affairs of the banks and thereby facilitated the raising of additional capital.

A noteworthy development, during reasonably prosperous times, was the establishment in Cork of the Munster Bank in 1864. It embarked on a rapid expansion of branches, mainly in the southern region of the country, and in 1870 established a presence in Dublin when it merged with the La Touche, one of the few remaining private banks. It tended to concentrate on the agricultural

community and operated with a relatively high ratio of lendings to deposits. This left the bank exposed, especially when it became known that interest on relatively large unsecured advances to major shareholders was not being paid, and it had to rely on the Bank of Ireland for temporary assistance. With a further deterioration in the financial condition of the Munster Bank, the Bank of Ireland decided to put a limit on the growing amount of credit it was prepared to grant and indicated that it would not continue to honour its cheques if that were to result in the limit being exceeded.

Against this background, the Munster Bank closed its doors in 1885. This led to questions in Parliament and to an exchange of correspondence between the Bank of Ireland and the Chancellor of the Exchequer, in which the Bank of Ireland was reminded of its privileges and its associated responsibilities. Later that year, arrangements were made to raise capital locally, which culminated in the incorporation with limited liability of a new major bank with head office in Cork. Thus was the Munster and Leinster Bank established in 1885, with Catholic support. It took over the assets, without any loss to its existing depositors, of the Munster Bank, some twenty years after it was initially launched. However, the shareholders of the Munster Bank had to forfeit their capital in order to meet the deficiencies that had arisen in the assets of that failed bank.

The newly established Munster and Leinster was enthusiastically supported by the local community. It pursued a conservative lending policy, which gave it a relatively high ratio of liquid or readily encashable assets to deposits. It also competed vigorously for new accounts, especially those of local authorities. After concentrating on the provinces of Munster and Leinster for some forty years, it set out to become a countrywide bank, establishing its first branch in Belfast in 1918. It did not, however, have the right to issue its own currency notes, since banks established after 1845 were prohibited from doing so.

The Post Office Savings Bank, with its ready-made nationwide outlets even in remote areas, was established by the government in 1861. By 1885, its deposits exceeded those of the trustee savings banks. This initiative was taken partly because of concern that had existed since the 1840s about the stability of the savings banks and which was reflected in their reducing level of deposits since 1844. All of the deposits placed in the Post Office Savings Bank and the trustee savings banks were invested abroad in British government paper until the late 1930s, when the first steps were taken to convert the savings banks' foreign assets into Irish government securities.

This process, which was interrupted in the 1940s when there were substantial increases in the foreign assets of the savings banks, continued through the 1950s and 1960s and was not completed until 1969, when the remaining foreign assets of the banking system were being transferred to the Central Bank. The Post Office Savings Bank recorded steady progress up to the 1960s, especially in the 1940s, in competition with the clearing banks, particularly in rural areas without ready access to such banks.

There are currently nine building societies in Ireland, four of which were established in the period 1861 to 1883, two in the 1930s, one in the mid-1950s and two during the 1970s. The building societies, however, were not destined to play a significant part in the Irish financial sector until the 1960s. This reflected the dominance of the rural sector in the Irish economy until recent decades and the limited scope, until relatively recently, for financing the personal acquisition of marketable, privately owned dwellings.

Guinness & Mahon, the only private banking partnership to maintain its individual identity, was established in 1836 and it was not until 1966 that it was converted into a limited company. The founding families of Guinness & Mahon also penetrated the London financial scene in the 1880s and established a successful merchant banking business in the City which, in more recent times, became the parent or owner of its Dublin-based sister bank. In 1989, the Bank of Yokohama became the ultimate dominant shareholder of Guinness & Mahon.

The basic structure of Irish banking was to remain unchanged from 1885 up to the 1960s. The only significant structural change to occur in the meantime was the takeovers in 1917 of the Belfast Banking Company by the Midland Bank and of the Ulster Bank by the National Westminster Bank. Sizeable amalgamations between major banks had been occurring around the same time in British banking, a development that was officially discouraged in 1918.

In 1919, the Dáil established the National Land Bank, which was taken over by the Bank of Ireland in 1926 and renamed the National City Bank in 1927. Some forty years later, in 1968, Chase Manhattan Bank purchased a major stake in this bank and its name was changed to Chase and Bank of Ireland (International) Limited, before being fully absorbed into the Chase Bank (Ireland) Limited in 1979 — a bank that has scaled down its operations significantly since the mid-1980s. In 1923, shortly after the Irish Free State was established, the Royal Bank of Ireland exchanged its branches in Northern Ireland for those of the Belfast Banking Company in the Republic, thereby reducing competition in banking in both areas. Furthermore, in the 1920s, the registers of British government stock held by Northern Ireland residents were transferred from the head office of the Bank of Ireland to its main branch in Belfast.

No further significant structural change in banking was to occur until the late 1950s, apart from the transferring of the head office of the Provincial Bank from London to Dublin in 1953. The head office of the National Bank was never transferred from London to Dublin, since such a move would have resulted in the loss of its London clearing bank status.

A striking feature of the evolution of the Irish banking industry over the centuries is the extent to which it corresponded with what was occurring in Scottish and English banking. This may be attributed to two different, but supportive influences. The first was the extent to which knowledge, technique and experience were being transferred across national boundaries independently of the authorities, facilitated by the fixed rate of exchange and no barriers to capital movements between Ireland, Scotland and England.

The second and probably more important influence was the legislative and policy initiatives that were taken. Before the Act of Union in 1801, legislation and policy relating to banking were different in Ireland to that in Scotland and England. There was strong resistance in Ireland to the spread of British influence over Irish banking. This delayed for many decades the emergence in Ireland of what is nowadays known as central banking functions, which were eventually introduced mainly as a result of imbalances in the fiscal finances in Ireland in the aftermath of the American Declaration of Independence in 1776. Other legislative initiatives affecting banking in Ireland in the eighteenth century also seemed to be concerned primarily with Irish problems, for example discouraging merchants engaged in foreign trade from becoming involved in the banking business.

Following the Act of Union, there was a significant shift in the direction of policy and legislation. From that time on, Irish banking followed very closely what was happening in the United Kingdom, especially in the first half of the nineteenth century. Monetary and banking reforms, together with supporting legislative changes introduced in the UK after the Napoleonic wars, were extended without resistance to Ireland. Similarly, in the 1840s, monetary control was extended over banking in Britain and in Ireland when the central position of the Bank of England was strengthened in England at the same time as that of the Bank of Ireland was weakened in Ireland.

By the 1840s, it was clear that the British authorities did not envisage the emergence of a central bank in Ireland with a monopoly of the note issue. After 1845, apart from the Bills of Exchange Act 1882 (legislation which concerned the conduct of banking business from a commercial viewpoint), there were no substantive changes for seventy years in monetary and banking legislation either in Britain or Ireland. Significant legislative changes in Irish banking were not to occur until the late 1920s.

There was a high degree of confidence in Irish banking over the past two centuries and the basic banking services provided in Ireland were of a similar quality to those available abroad, especially in Scotland and England. By international standards, Irish banking was a safe haven for savings, especially since the holders of the currency notes issued by banks and their depositors (as distinct from shareholders) did not experience significant losses in the event of bank failures. However, in instances where depositors did experience some losses through the failure of very small banks, the authorities — in pursuing the policy objective of the times, of placing full responsibility for the management of risk with the private investors — did not become involved in providing funds to rescue the ailing banks or to compensate their depositors. The only exception in Ireland occurred in 1977, when the Exchequer contributed less than £1 million to the depositors of a small local bank (the Irish Trust Bank) that went into liquidation in 1976. Furthermore, no losses have been experienced over the years by those who placed their savings with building societies. Efficient arrangements for making payments have prevailed in Ireland, especially since the disappearance of the shortage of coinage after the Napoleonic wars. Innovations were also introduced into Irish banking without much delay, particularly from the 1820s onwards in a commercial environment that did not rely on the state for support. Furthermore, the real purchasing power of money over the past 200 years was not seriously eroded by rising prices in peacetime conditions until the inflationary experiences of recent decades.

FINANCIAL INNOVATION:
1820s TO 1950s

The four most important financial innovations in Irish banking during the last century were the institution of arrangements for exchanging currency notes between banks; the introduction of clearing facilities for cheques; the emergence of the secured overdraft facility at a time when a growing proportion of firms were adopting limited liability status; and the bringing of banking to the customer by establishing bank branches in local towns throughout the country. These innovations reflected the demands for savings and payments facilities and for seasonal and long-term credit.

Currency notes in circulation increased significantly between 1800 and 1845 — from almost £3 million to £6.4 million. A limit was then placed on the issue of currency notes by banks unless backed by gold or silver, provided the silver did not exceed one quarter of the amount of gold. One major innovation that emerged from the growth in the circulation of bank notes was the establishment, by private initiative, of an arrangement between the banks for the clearing or exchanging of one another's notes. The rise in the circulation of currency notes issued by the Bank of Ireland and the emerging joint stock banks, with their own note issues and growing branch networks, led to cooperation and the establishment of a bank note exchange between the banks in 1825 under the auspices of the Bank of Ireland.

As the banking system developed and grew in confidence, it introduced another major innovation for the purposes of making payments. This was the cheque. It was to prove more convenient and safer than notes and coin for discharging large payments. Banks also found it more profitable to provide cheques than to issue currency notes. This was because the banks' current account liabilities, against which the cheques were drawn, could be partly supported by relatively high yielding assets rather than with non-interest yielding gold and silver

TILL MONEY
The stock of notes and coins that is maintained by a bank at its branches to meet its customers' over-the-counter withdrawals. Also known as 'vault cash'.

Today, with the growth in the use of cheques and computerised payments, 'till money' must be supported with other encashable assets available to settle payments made by cheques or telephonic instructions.

coins, with which issues of currency notes had to be matched after 1845.

As early as 1845, another private innovation requiring cooperation between competitors, again organised under the leadership of the Bank of Ireland, took place when facilities for the exchanging or clearing of cheques between the banks were established. However, the very small increase in the currency notes issued by the Irish banks (from £6.4 million in 1845 to £6.7 million in 1900) was probably more associated with the scope provided for an increase in the amount of British currency, including sovereigns, in circulation rather than with the growing popularity of cheques for effecting payments.

Those banks with the right to issue notes were able to carry their normal level of till money free of interest costs. They accomplished this by maintaining their own note issue in line with the amount of till money (in the form of gold and silver coins) they considered necessary to support their scale of business. If they increased the circulation of their own notes to a level that required them to hold gold and silver coins in excess of normal till money requirements, they would not be adding to their profits. This experience discouraged banks from issuing their own notes beyond a certain point (that is, the level of till money required for operational purposes), with the result that bank deposits and British currency notes acquired a more prominent position. These arrangements led to bank deposits, including those with the Post Office Savings Bank, sovereigns and British currency notes rising as a proportion of savers' portfolios at the expense of Irish bank notes.

Deposits with banks, which consisted mainly of savings rather than balances for effecting payments and which were probably the dominant liquid or encashable component of wealth, increased from about £8 million in 1850 to some £43 million in 1900. Savings were also being accumulated with the savings banks, particularly the Post Office Savings Bank, which in 1900 aggregated to some £10.5

million compared with £3 million in 1845. No data are available on the magnitude of the rise in the circulation of coins, including sovereigns, and Bank of England notes, between the 1840s and the early 1900s — a period during which the economy was growing at some 0.7 per cent a year.

By reference to the amount of the gold coinage withdrawn during the early years of World War I, the indications are that the value of the circulation of gold coinage at the beginning of the war may not have been far short of that of the Irish bank notes in circulation. The subsequent experiences of the late 1920s, with the substitution of new Irish currencies for the note issue of the Irish banks and also for British currency in circulation, suggest that the amount of Bank of England notes then in circulation may have been about one and a half times that of the active Irish bank note circulation. One could conclude that the circulation of Bank of England notes in Ireland prior to 1914 may not have been much in excess of the aggregate circulation of gold coins and Irish bank notes.

Another major innovation in banking was the development of the overdraft method of lending. While this had been a feature of banking since the 1820s, it did not become popular until the last quarter of the nineteenth century when the advantages of the secured overdraft became more widely appreciated, at a time when a growing number of firms were adopting limited liability. The specialised financing needs of industry that emerged in other countries, in the form of merchant and investment banking, never became a strong feature of Irish banking. This was because of the continuance of the strong agricultural base to the Irish economy, the absence of a dynamic corporate sector and the direct links of large transport, manufacturing and trading firms with the London capital and financial markets.

Apart from the emergence of stockbroking partnerships towards the end of the eighteenth century and the gradual evolution of the stock exchanges since then, there have been no significant innovative developments in the financial markets in Ireland until recent times. This was because of the relatively low level of government borrowing until recent decades, the centring by the banks of their external assets on London, primarily in liquid form, and because the total amount of capital raised by issues of equity on the stock exchanges in Ireland was not substantial. A feature of the sterling area was that it discouraged the development of national financial markets. It centred both the accumulation of liquid assets by financial institutions and the large-scale borrowings of governments and major corporations on the internationally-oriented institutions and markets located in London.

At local level, the banks penetrated the growing retail market for banking facilities by continuing to extend their branch network throughout the country from the 1820s up to the early 1920s. This development also reflected inter-bank competition to meet the growing demands in local towns for bank services, especially depository and cashing facilities. Close on 130 branches were opened in the decade 1826 to 1836. Fewer branches were established between 1836 and 1860 when the number increased by only 50 to around 180, reflecting the effects of the Famine and static economic conditions in Ireland. Over the next two relatively prosperous decades, up to 1880, some 300 branches were established. This was followed by a rise to 660 in 1900, mainly by way of sub-office expansion in sluggish economic circumstances.

Competition in establishing branches became intense after 1900. During the disturbed, but exceptionally prosperous (especially for agriculture) two decades up to 1920, the number of branches almost doubled to around a figure of 1,260 in 1920. This proliferation of branches was associated with a more than four-fold increase in the amount of savings held with the banks. At the same time, currency notes issued by the Irish banks rose from £6.7 million in 1900 to £26.6 million in 1920. Much of this increase occurred during the period 1914 to 1920, when sovereigns were being withdrawn, and

INFLATION

A fall in the value or overall purchasing power of money owing to a general rise in the prices of goods and services. An inflationary policy is one that leads to such a fall in the value of money. Inflation is usually associated with a depreciation of the rate of exchange of a country's currency relative to other currencies.

the currency notes were enjoying legal tender status. Prices, too, were increasing rapidly — by 150 per cent over the same six-year period — this being the first major bout of inflation since the Napoleonic wars, one hundred years earlier.

Deposits with the clearing banks increased more evenly during these decades, from £43 million in 1900 to £183 million in 1920. The savings banks, because of strong competition from the numerous new branches of the clearing banks, experienced a more modest rate of expansion in the twenty years to 1920, when their deposits increased by £7 million to £17.5 million. The extension of branch banking over the nineteenth and early twentieth centuries enabled the banks to diversify their sources of funds and lending portfolios, and avoided the establishment of a large number of small local banks with relatively risky lending portfolios. This contributed to the high degree of stability of banking in Ireland over the past 150 years or so and reduced the number of bank failures and abortive mergers that otherwise would have occurred.

The boom in banking activity over the first two decades of this century came to a sudden halt in the early 1920s. A contraction in the level of deposits with banks was experienced during the 1920s and 1930s, when prices, particularly of agricultural products, fell sharply. In addition, a consensus emerged that a number of towns had too many branches, which led to a small reduction in the branch network, particularly during the 1940s. However, deposits with banks began to increase again from the early 1940s onwards as a result of the impact of World War II. This resulted in a severe contraction in imports, higher prices for agricultural exports and a substantial balance of payments surplus during the first half of the 1940s.

Bank deposits, including those with the Northern Ireland banks, increased by some £300 million over the twenty-year period 1940 to 1960. It is estimated that deposits throughout Ireland with the savings banks (which had recorded little change between the early 1920s and late 1930s) also rose during the

1940s and 1950s, by around £140 million to a level of £160 million in 1960. This represented a much higher rate of growth in funds placed with the savings banks — the opposite to what was experienced in the previous expansion between 1900 and 1920. The more prominent position of the savings banks in the mid-decades of this century may be attributed to the fact that the branch network of the clearing banks was being reduced, rather than extended, at that time, thereby enabling the savings banks to capture a larger share of the market.

Since 1960, there have been major structural changes in the financial sector, both in the Republic and in Northern Ireland, with the building societies and subsidiaries of the clearing banks coming to the fore at the expense of the public sector institutions, especially the Post Office Savings Bank. Since statistics about a number of the financial activities or institutions in Northern Ireland are not shown separately from aggregate UK data since 1983, it is not possible to quantify with confidence the relative sizes of the different categories of financial institutions in Northern Ireland in the 1980s.

In addition, comparisons between Northern Ireland's financial institutions and those in the Republic are more difficult to make nowadays because of the fluctuations in the exchange rate between the Irish pound and sterling. As regards the branch network, a further small reduction in the number of offices has occurred since the 1960s, especially in the Republic, giving a level of 682 at the end of 1988. While the amalgamations of the banks and the advent of the 'travelling bank' gave scope for the closing of non-profitable branches in rural areas, this was partly offset by the need to establish branches in the rapidly expanding urban areas.

CENTRAL BANKING:
AFTER INDEPENDENCE

The most significant changes in Irish banking in this century are, firstly, the reinstatement of the Irish currency and the establishment of the Currency Commission/Central Bank of Ireland following political independence in the early 1920s; secondly, the structural changes in banking from the 1960s onwards; and, thirdly, the implications of the breaking of the fixed link between the Irish pound and sterling in 1979.

When the state was founded in the early 1920s, the per capita level of income in Ireland compared favourably with that in many European countries. Ireland also had a relatively advanced banking system that was fully integrated into the sterling area and held ample liquidity in the form of sterling balances. One of the main characteristics of membership of the sterling area was the free movement of capital at internationally competitive rates of interest, not only between Ireland and the UK but also with the rest of the sterling area. Moreover, as far as the countries of the sterling area were concerned, there was free movement of capital from them to the rest of the world.

Another significant feature was that the London financial institutions and markets acted as the lender of last resort to the banks in the member-countries of the sterling area. In the eighteenth century, private Irish banks had correspondent associations with banks in London. During the first half of the last century, the Bank of Ireland could rely on temporary support from the Bank of England, not only on its own behalf but indirectly on behalf of other Irish banks that found it necessary to have resort to the Bank of Ireland rather than going directly themselves to London.

As the nineteenth century progressed, Irish banks relied less on the Bank of Ireland for temporary accommodation as they themselves began to accumulate sterling liquid assets and British government securities and to centre the management of their growing liquidity on London. The Irish banks' liquid balances in London increased when external trade grew more rapidly than the rest of the economy; when lending opportunities in Ireland were not attractive, as in the 1880s and 1890s; when outflows associated with the servicing of past British investment in Irish railways and the transfer of annual land rents abroad tapered off from the 1880s onwards; and when agricultural exports prospered, especially during the two world wars. As recently as 1950, half of the savings placed with banks were held abroad in the form of short-term balances with financial institutions and marketable British government securities. Apart from the clearing banks, the other domestic financial institutions and personal savers also channelled funds into British government securities and equities quoted on the London Stock Exchange.

Another hallmark of the sterling area was the existence of fixed rates of exchange between member currencies, which led to sterling being accepted without question for making payments and acting as a store of value throughout the sterling area. In the 1920s, British currency notes and coins circulated freely in Ireland, as they had for the past one hundred years. The notes, which were never legal tender in Ireland, circulated alongside the currency notes issued by the Irish banks and were automatically exchangeable at par with the Irish bank notes, which also did not have legal tender status except during the period 1914 to 1919. British sovereigns, which were the only form of legal tender in Ireland since the 1820s, had virtually disappeared from active circulation since the early years of World War I; those that remained in private possession were regarded as valuables or part of wealth rather than means for making payments.

The banks throughout Ireland experienced a very rapid rate of growth in the three-year period 1918 to 1921, when their lending rose by £50 million, or 100 per cent, and their deposits by £80 million, or some 60 per cent. This expansion was probably associated with restocking and replacement after the

*CLEARING AND
SETTLEMENT
ARRANGEMENTS
Cooperative
arrangements between
banks and similar
institutions that
specialise in the clearing
of cheques, whereby
they offset their cheques
against one another
before making the net
payments. Such
arrangements also exist
between banks for
electronically
communicated payment
instructions.*

*The Stock Exchange
also has clearing and
settlement arrangements
for facilitating transfers
of ownership of gilts
and equities.*

*With the rapid
growth in financial
transactions, especially
across national frontiers,
central banks are
becoming more involved
with clearing and
settlement systems to
ensure that they
continue to operate
efficiently.*

war. Over the next four years to the end of 1925, the banks' lending remained more or less stable, while their deposits fell by some £30 million, or nearly 15 per cent, as prices unwound and as the economy slowed down in the aftermath of war. The banks' deposit accounts and to a lesser extent their lending continued to contract, but more modestly, during the second half of the 1920s and also in the 1930s, before recovering in the 1940s and increasing thereafter, at times excessively. No data are available to facilitate a comparison between the experiences in the Republic and Northern Ireland during the 1920s, but it is probable that there was a contraction in the role played by the banks in both areas, as had also been occurring in Britain during the 1920s.

The use of bank cheques and accompanying arrangements for exchanging them and settling the net differences between banks had also been a well-established feature of Irish banking from as far back as the 1840s. Thus, in the 1920s, Ireland had a highly efficient cheque-payments system by international standards, both in terms of the costs of cheque transactions and the length of time before they were presented for payment. It extended not only throughout Ireland, but was also fully integrated into the domestic and international cheque clearing and settlement arrangements of the UK clearing banks. Up to the late 1920s, deposits with the clearing banks (that is, the banks that provided cheque-payment facilities to their customers) and the savings banks in Ireland were also regarded as being expressed in sterling.

When Ireland became independent again, it is not surprising that the authorities were slow to disturb the efficient payments arrangements that existed not only within the country but also for over 90 per cent of the country's international trade and virtually all of its external capital transactions. There was also widespread confidence, by both residents and the recently designated non-residents in Northern Ireland and Britain, in the currency in circulation and in bank deposits, whose real purchasing power was increasing in the 1920s

Coins introduced in 1928

because of declining prices. The authorities were most anxious to preserve this confidence, especially in view of the international concern in the early 1920s about the effects of hyper-inflation in continental Europe. The existing arrangements offered the prospect of continuity in the efficient payments facilities and in the stability of the value of the currency. This was to be welcomed in the less buoyant economic circumstances of the 1920s, compared with the relatively prosperous conditions, especially in rural Ireland, in the opening decades of the century which reached a peak during World War I when prices rose substantially.

After careful consideration of the reports of a commission appointed in the spring of 1926, the government decided in 1927 that it would be in the national interest to effect two significant reforms — one to reinstate legally the Irish pound, the other to introduce into circulation a distinctive set of Irish notes and coins. These reforms were to be introduced only on the clear understanding that there would be no exchange controls between Ireland and Britain, and that the Saorstát pound would exchange on a one-for-one, no-margins basis with the pound sterling. This meant that there would be no change whatsoever in the value or purchasing power, in terms of sterling, of the currency and bank deposits. From the legal viewpoint, however, the reforms provided for the establishment of a different currency in the Republic from that in Northern Ireland and Britain. In practice, the new Irish notes and coins were quickly accepted into circulation and became, in the words of Yeats, 'the silent ambassadors of national taste'.

The Currency Act 1927 declared that the standard unit of value shall be the Saorstát pound, later to be described as the Irish pound in 1937. The Act also prescribed under Section 10 that every contract, etc. effected after the Irish pound came into circulation shall be made in terms of money that is legal tender in the country, unless the contract, etc. is expressed in the currency of another country other than the Irish state. This statutory provision

William Butler Yeats chaired the committee set up in 1926 to recommend designs for a new series of Irish coins. Ireland's issue, in 1928, of an entire new coinage was the first by a modern state. In 1939, the words 'Saorstát Éireann' were changed to 'Éire'

is now incorporated in the Central Bank Act 1989.

The provisions of the Currency Act became effective in 1928, with the introduction of the Irish legal tender notes and the Irish coinage in substitution for the British currency, which continued to circulate freely but without legal underpinning. However, it was not until the 1970s, when fixed exchange rates became the exception in the world and the fixed link with sterling was being questioned, that the banks began to clarify for their customers that their deposits were expressed in Irish pounds unless otherwise specified.

The other major reform undertaken in 1927 was to establish institutional arrangements to manage the Irish currency and to ensure that it would continue to be backed 100 per cent by sterling. It was also envisaged that the new arrangements would avoid the extension of interest-free credit to Britain, which followed automatically from the circulation of British currency in Ireland. The retention in Ireland of British currency for the purposes of effecting domestic payments was equivalent to the holding of British government paper on which no interest or dividend was directly received. It made economic sense to incur the expense of providing Irish currency, since this cost would be only a fraction of the earnings from abroad on the sterling backing for the Irish currency.

The new institutional arrangements to give effect to these reforms led to the establishment of the

Legal tender notes were introduced in 1928, adorned by a female figure, symbolic of the new Irish state. This was based on a painting by Sir John Lavery and now features on the watermark of the current notes

Currency Commission in 1927. This institution — the forerunner of the Central Bank of Ireland — was made responsible for introducing the newly designed Irish notes and coins in exchange for British currency, which was repatriated. This enabled the Currency Commission to provide a 100 per cent sterling backing for the Irish currency by acquiring sterling assets on which interest was earned. Initially, the circulation of Irish currency rose rapidly to the level of £6.5 million in 1929 and then recorded a modest increase of around £0.5 million over the next five years.

The experience of introducing the new Irish notes into circulation suggests that the amount of British currency notes in circulation in Ireland was not significantly in excess of the amount of currency notes that had been issued by the Irish banks. As increases in Irish currency in circulation began to exceed the amount of sterling repatriated, the Currency Commission continued to accumulate sterling assets to back the issues of Irish currency. Such excess issues of Irish currency were only made available to the banks in exchange for sterling balances in London. The reforms of the late 1920s set the legal background for the gradual distancing of the management of Irish monetary affairs from that of Britain. This, however, did not gain momentum for a number of decades by which time economic circumstances, especially international monetary relations, had changed significantly.

With the introduction of legal tender notes, the clearing banks were no longer permitted to issue their own currency notes, of which there was about £6.5 million in circulation in 1929. In addition, they had to pay interest to the Currency Commission on their notes that remained in circulation. This gave an incentive to the five banks concerned to withdraw their notes and replace them with legal tender notes. The interest payments also helped to compensate the Currency Commission for the loss of income arising from the lower circulation of its legal tender notes.

The banks were partly cushioned from the effects

CENTRAL BANK
The national monetary authority responsible for the formulation and implementation of monetary policy, management of the exchange rate and official external reserves, provision of notes and coins, and supervision of banks, building societies, other financial institutions and the financial and capital markets. The Exchequer Account, Gilts Registers and Gilts Settlement Office are also maintained at and operated by the Central Bank.

Specimen of the ploughman note, circulated in 1929-53

of this development for a time. As their currency notes were being withdrawn, each of the clearing banks was permitted to place in circulation a limited amount of quasi-private currency notes bearing its own name. These hybrid notes were called Consolidated Bank Notes (better known as 'ploughman' notes since they featured a ploughman on the front) and were provided by the Currency Commission. But they were not legal tender. An upper limit of £6 million was placed on their total circulation, which grew rapidly to around £4.5 million in 1931, thereby replacing within a year or so some two-thirds of the old currency notes that ceased to be issued by the banks in 1929. Interest was also paid by the banks to the Currency Commission on these notes, which reduced their attractiveness to the banks but made a contribution to the Currency Commission to offset its losses from not having the opportunity to issue additional legal tender notes. The circulation of Consolidated Bank Notes never reached the maximum limit of £6 million and this transitional arrangement was terminated in 1953.

The next significant structural development in Irish banking after the late 1920s was the formal establishment of the Central Bank of Ireland early in 1943. This followed a major evaluation of Irish

banking by a commission appointed in 1934 and which reported in 1938. While central banking was firmly established in most European countries during the last century, the worldwide emergence of central banks is mainly a feature of the twentieth century and was associated with the international trend towards nationalism and independence. Given these trends, especially in the British Commonwealth after World War I, it is not surprising that a central bank was established in Ireland in the early 1940s, although it was not obvious at the time what a central bank could hope to achieve in addition to the functions already being performed by the Currency Commission.

The Central Bank was made responsible not only for the functions of the Currency Commission, but also for the duties and powers conferred on it by the Central Bank Act, 1942. Under this Act, the Central Bank was given the responsibility to guard the purchasing power of the currency and to control credit in the interest of the people as a whole. With the rapidly changing external monetary environment since the 1950s and also with the substantial increase in the role of the state, there has been a rapid rate of evolution in central banking in Ireland in recent decades.

The board of the newly established Central Bank met for the first time on 1 February 1943. The members were: (seated, left to right) David D. Coyle, Malachi Sweetman, John F. Punch, Joseph Brennan (Governor), William O'Brien, Timothy A. Smiddy; (standing, left to right) R. T. McGuinness (Secretary), Gabriel Brock, Rt Hon Lord Glenavy and James J. McElligott

NORTHERN IRELAND: CURRENCY IN CIRCULATION

Northern Ireland does not have an independent currency. Sterling has been in circulation there since 1826 and, unlike in the Republic, no steps were taken to replace it in the 1920s. As a result, there has been little change in the composition of the currency in circulation, except that the position became somewhat more complicated between the 1920s and 1980s with the percolation of Irish legal tender notes and coins into circulation there. Bank of England notes continue to be the main component of the note circulation. Each of the Northern Ireland banks still has the scope to issue its own currency notes nor is it uncommon to find Scottish bank notes in circulation.

In 1929, six of the clearing banks then operating in Northern Ireland, which had the right to issue their own private currency notes since before 1845, were allowed to continue with this practice and retain some of the profits arising from the issue of these notes at the expense of the authorities. The note issue of the clearing banks must be backed, but not on a daily basis, with Bank of England notes (and coins) or non-interest balances with the Bank of England. While the circulation of the Northern Ireland bank notes continues to increase, especially since the mid-1980s (amounting to nearly £300 million in 1989), it has not displaced the dominant position held by Bank of England notes. In the event of a relatively rapid growth of the Northern Ireland bank note issue, the counterpart arrangements with the Bank of England would be unlikely to be sufficiently remunerative to meet the production and management costs of a substantially increased circulation of private bank notes in Northern Ireland that threatened to displace, to a significant extent, Bank of England notes from circulation.

About 20 per cent of the total note circulation in Northern Ireland consists of bank notes issued by the banks, with Bank of England notes accounting for most of the remaining 80 per cent. This would suggest that the circulation of Bank of England notes in Northern Ireland amounted to an estimated £1,200 million in 1989. It may be only profitable for the banks to issue their own notes up to an amount approximately equal to the amount of Bank of England notes and balances with the Bank of England that they must hold to support their normal day-to-day banking business. Apart from Scotland and Hong Kong, where all the profits of the private bank note issue are channelled to the authorities, Northern Ireland is one of the few remaining places in the world where banks are allowed to issue their own private currency notes.

The substitution of Bank of England notes for the existing private note issue of the Northern Ireland banks would result in an increase in the interest-free loan to the British authorities that arises from the circulation of Bank of England notes in Northern Ireland. But there would also be a reduction in the interest-free liabilities of the Bank of England to the Northern Ireland banks. However, the Northern Ireland banks would respond to such developments by changing the composition of their deposits, liquid assets and loans. Such changes would eventually result in a small reduction in their profitability and perhaps some contraction in market share.

The indications are that, since the break in the link with sterling in 1979, Irish legal tender notes are rarely used for the purposes of effecting payments between residents of Northern Ireland. Similarly, Irish coinage virtually disappeared from circulation in Northern Ireland in the early 1980s.

PART II

DEVELOPMENTS
SINCE THE 1960s

CLEARING BANKS:
STRUCTURAL CHANGES

To commemorate the 50th anniversary of the 1916 Rising, a silver coin was struck in 1966, with a value of ten shillings. Pádraig Pearse is featured on the obverse, with the legendary Irish hero, Cuchulainn, on the reverse.

Throughout the world, banking and securities markets were reasonably international in character during the nineteenth century, within the constraints set by the technical limitations on communications. This was due to the open characteristics of the gold standard and the world-wide influence of the European colonial powers. Banking in Europe, in particular, had been transformed from small regional partnerships into major national and international banking institutions with headquarters in the capitals of the colonial powers.

However, the first sixty years or so of this century saw a change of direction at world level. Countries were concentrating on maintaining the stability of their own local banking and financial structures, with less emphasis on the multinational scene. But for the past twenty-five years, banking and financial markets throughout the world have again become international in orientation and have been straddling national frontiers. This development was led by the major US banking institutions in the 1960s and 1970s in their drive to establish a worldwide presence. At the same time, European banks were also consolidating their international representation and, in the 1980s, the Japanese banks established themselves as the foremost force internationally.

This renewed emphasis on multinational banking and internationally integrated financial markets over the past twenty-five years was reflected in Irish banking and encouraged major structural changes — indeed, the first to have occurred in this century. Generally, the banking industry tends towards concentration into larger institutions by way of horizontal mergers, presumably to reap economies of scale by increasing market share. This occurred in Ireland during the 1960s, when mergers halved the number of clearing banks from eight to four and resulted in the establishment of two major Irish-owned banking groups. This period of mergers can be regarded as part of the process by which Irish banking strengthened itself to cope with the threat of external takeovers and increased competition from abroad, and embarked on the pursuit of economies of scale within the Irish banking market.

The Bank of Ireland consolidated its position within Ireland when it took over the Hibernian Bank in 1958 and the Irish branches of the National Bank in 1965 (the branches of the National Bank located in England, including those in the City, being sold to a major Scottish clearing bank). The following year, 1966, Allied Irish Bank was founded through the merger of three banks: the Munster and Leinster Bank, the Provincial Bank of Ireland and the Royal Bank of Ireland.

NON-CLEARING BANKS
Not engaged in providing personal cheque-account facilities, these banks (also known as non-associated banks) engage in wholesale, merchant and industrial banking. Wholesale banks concentrate on borrowing or lending large amounts, with most of their business being transacted with other banks, other financial institutions and major corporate clients. Merchant banks are a specialised form of wholesale bank; their business includes underwriting and raising capital for firms and governments, managing clients' funds and advising on mergers and takeovers. Industrial banks concentrate on extending instalment credit facilities and leasing to medium-sized and smaller customers.

COMPETITION FROM ABROAD

In the mid-1960s, the Irish banking industry was dominated by the clearing banks, which accounted for some 70 per cent of the total market for short-term savings. These banks operated a cartel and entry into retail banking was inhibited other than by way of a takeover.

On the other hand, there was virtually no control over the establishment of branches or subsidiaries of foreign banks that wished to concentrate on non-clearing or wholesale banking. In the ten years to 1975, major banks from North America and Europe quickly established themselves in Ireland and helped to create a more competitive climate within the banking industry.

North American banks established their presence in the second half of the 1960s and, by the early 1970s, five major banks from this region were in operation and had acquired over 5 per cent of the banking market. Since then, these banks have scaled down their activities and have experienced a reduction (to around 4 per cent) in their share of domestic banking in Ireland, especially since 1985. This mainly reflects a change of emphasis by a number of major US banks. In the light of the international debt crisis of the 1980s and the tightening of profit margins in banking both domestically and internationally, some US banks are withdrawing from widespread representation around the globe and concentrating on the major international financial centres and the US domestic scene.

This wave of external interest from North America was followed by the entry of a number of banks from EC member-states during the first half of the 1970s and again in the early 1980s. By this stage, entry into banking was regulated by the Central Bank, under the bank-licensing and supervisory powers conferred on it by the 1971 Central Bank Act. The share of domestic banking conducted by the EC banks has continued to increase from 2 per cent in 1971 to nearly 10 per cent in the late 1980s, despite the withdrawal during 1987 and 1988 of a few EC banks from their interests in Ireland.

Irish banking has also been open over the centuries to external competition from foreign banks that did not have a physical presence in Ireland. Nowadays, foreign banks from major international financial centres, including Japanese banks, compete directly with banks in Ireland in providing credit facilities, not only to the public sector but also to the larger corporate borrowers. While the data on total borrowing (net) by Irish residents from external banks without a presence in Ireland are not comprehensive, they suggest that there is a reasonable degree of competition from this source. Even in the 1980s, as international banks became more cautious about extending credit across international frontiers, the magnitude of direct lending from abroad to the private sector remained close to about one-tenth of total private sector borrowing from banks within the country.

This suggests that the establishment of the single banking market throughout Europe may not have as large an effect on the availability and cost of bank credit in Ireland as some expect. Nevertheless, as a result of the creation of a single financial market in Europe, a greater range of more competitive savings facilities will probably be made available in the next decade, not only by the credit institutions located in Ireland but also by those situated in other European countries.

Although the share of foreign banks located in Ireland in the domestic banking market has not been increasing (remaining in the region of nearly 15 per cent), these banks continue to be an important competitive force, especially in relation to non-retail or wholesale banking. A significant part of their business is the provision of foreign currency loans to corporate borrowers at rates determined in highly competitive international markets. This brings the forces of international competition to bear on local banking, which would lose its narrow-margin business to foreign banks if it did not remain internationally competitive.

The clearing bank groups — Allied Irish Bank, Bank of Ireland, National Irish Bank and Ulster Bank — successfully adapted themselves to these external forces. While retaining overdraft facilities, they introduced term-lending in 1972, established specialised subsidiaries and become involved in the inter-bank market. These policies are reflected in the size of the total business of the clearing banks, comprising their retail, merchant and industrial activities, which has fluctuated between 83 and 86 per cent of the total domestic banking market since the early 1970s. Two major initiatives by the clearing banks — a reduction in their numbers through mergers (from eight to four) and the establishment of subsidiaries on a decartelised basis in the rapidly expanding areas of the banking market — enabled them to maintain their share of the banking market throughout the 1970s and increase it in the second half of the 1980s.

The instalment-credit banking subsidiaries of the Irish clearing banks were established at the turn of the 1960s to compete with the subsidiaries of existing UK institutions in the growing instalment-credit and leasing markets. They were also established with a view to retaining as many as possible of the benefits of the cartel by the clearing banks themselves, by confining the payment of relatively high rates of interest to the personal and medium-sized corporate deposits that were switched to their instalment-credit subsidiaries.

Steps were then taken by the clearing banks in the mid-1960s to gain a foothold in the rapidly growing wholesale banking area when, with support primarily from UK merchant banks, they established merchant banking subsidiaries. Apart from competing with banks abroad, the establishment of subsidiaries outside the clearing banks' cartel also helped to increase competition between the clearing banks themselves, mainly via their subsidiaries. It is also of interest that the smaller Irish-based banks were established or incorporated since the late 1950s.

The strategy pursued by the clearing banks enabled them to capture the major share of the non-clearing banking business. By 1975, the subsidiaries of the clearing banks accounted for 47 per cent of the rapidly growing business of all the non-clearing banks — a proportion that has increased, especially since the mid-1980s, to 52 per cent at the end of June 1989.

Thus, exposure to external competition in banking helped to create a strong and competitive domestic base in Ireland, capable of confronting international competition with confidence. While it appears that the Irish banking industry has responded well to competition from abroad, the same conclusion cannot be reached in relation to its performance against other domestic deposit-taking and savings-collecting financial institutions. While competition from abroad tends to concentrate on major corporate clients, the challenge to the banks from domestic non-bank credit institutions for retail market share has been more penetrating. This was partly because of the latter's familiarity with the local scene and their relatively favourable tax treatment by the authorities. The traditional nature of retail banking products and services before the emergence of a more competitive retail banking climate since May 1985 (when each of the clearing banks was allowed to set independently its own structure of interest rates) may also have contributed to some loss of market share by the clearing banks.

SAVINGS BANKS AND BUILDING SOCIETIES

At the same time as foreign banks were being attracted to Ireland, an unprecedented degree of competition arose from non-bank, deposit-taking institutions within the country. However, the public sector institutions that compete directly with the banks for deposits have been losing out relative to the banks. (These institutions are the Post Office Savings Bank; the trustee savings banks, of which there are now two due to amalgamations in the 1980s, with head offices in Dublin and Cork; and the two state-sponsored financial institutions, the Agricultural Credit Corporation and the Industrial Credit Company.) The aggregate share of these institutions in the market for deposits fell from 20 per cent in 1965 to 10 per cent in 1985 — a proportion that has not changed significantly since then. This aggregate view does not reveal a small relative improvement in the position of the state-sponsored financial institutions and the trustee savings banks, which extended their branch networks since the 1960s. But the increased market share of these institutions has been more than offset by a major contraction in the role of the Post Office Savings Bank, from a 15 per cent share of the deposit market in 1965 to 3 per cent in recent years.

The story is quite different for the building societies, which responded to very favourable conditions between the mid-1960s and the mid-1980s. At the end of 1985, their shares and deposits accounted for 18 per cent of the total savings with deposit-taking financial institutions, compared with around 5 per cent in 1965, despite a substantial reduction in the number of societies to ten through rationalisation. There had been a very strong demand for mortgage finance between the mid-1960s and early 1980s, reflecting a growing population, a higher rate of marriage, rising incomes and a tax system that favoured investment in housing, especially in inflationary circumstances. The building societies responded enthusiastically by developing a five-fold increase in their branch and agency networks throughout the country, reaching 915 outlets (284 branches and 631 agencies) by the end of 1988. (The three protracted strikes in the clearing banks over the decade 1966 to 1976 gave support to this expansion.)

These developments resulted in a major increase in the role of the building societies in recent decades; their shares and deposits at the end of 1985 amounted to nearly half of the current and deposit accounts of the associated banks, compared with 7 per cent in 1965. Since 1986, however, the building societies have had to face more effective competition from the banks, a tightening of operating margins and pressure on market share. This is because of the phasing out of fiscal incentives and reporting requirements to the tax authorities that favoured the societies, the enhanced scope extended to building societies and clearing banks in setting their interest and mortgage rates, and the vigorous entry of the clearing banks into mortgage finance, which raised their share of total mortgage finance outstanding to around 22 per cent at the end of 1988.

In the wake of the 1973 oil crisis, the clearing banks became involved in providing temporary resources to the building societies in order to enable them to maintain their level of housing finance. Following an initiative by the Central Bank, and in anticipation of a tax incentive in the 1976 Budget, the clearing banks introduced their own facilities in the mid-1970s for extending mortgage credit for house purchase. Since the mid-1980s, the banks are much better poised to compete with the building societies, as the 1986 Budget placed banks in a more competitive position vis-à-vis the societies in the market for savings. Furthermore, since 1985 one bank — the Bank of Ireland — now owns the ICS Building Society.

With these developments, the building societies are now under pressure to retain their position in the overall savings and credit markets, especially in relation to the financing of housing. The societies' share of total mortgage finance outstanding at the end of 1988 was some 54 per cent compared with 57 per cent in 1985. It is also likely that the building societies will experience further competition in the 1990s for the financing of housing from external institutions as the single European financial market becomes a reality. However, under the 1989 Building Societies Act, it is envisaged that building societies will be given the opportunity to provide payments facilities, to extend credit for non-housing purposes and to provide, on an agency basis, a wide range of financial services. In this way, they will be able to compete on a wider front in the future with banks and other credit institutions. Moreover, since September 1989 the building societies are being supervised by the Central Bank, which has an even-handed approach to the supervision of all credit institutions. It is also of interest that the Central Bank will probably become responsible for the supervision of the trustee savings banks in 1990.

A noteworthy institutional development has been the spread of the credit union movement throughout the whole of Ireland since the 1960s. In 1988, it accounted for 3 to 4 per cent of total savings with deposit-taking institutions. (Building society shares and deposits accounted for a similar share in the early 1960s.) In 1989, there were nearly 500 individual credit unions in operation (400 in the Republic and 100 in Northern Ireland), with a total membership of about 850,000 and accumulated savings of nearly £600 million, of which an estimated £480 million related to the Republic.

Another institutional development of a financial nature is the emergence of a number of leasing companies, particularly in the late 1980s. These companies are raising funds by share issue, as well as borrowing, and are building up their share of the market in competition with the banks, the main providers of leasing facilities.

INSURANCE AND BANKING

INSURANCE
A contract between two parties whereby the insurer agrees to indemnify the insured upon the happening of a stipulated contingency. There is no certainty that the event for which the insurance policy is taken out will occur.

When one is not specifically referring to either assurance or insurance, the term 'insurance' embraces or relates to both businesses.

ASSURANCE
A contract, in exchange for a premium or premiums, to pay a person, or his/her representative, a sum of money at the end of a specified number of years or on the death of the person. Such contracts are known as assurance contracts, because the event (passage of time or death) for which the policy is taken out will definitely take place. Some assurance policies may be regarded as forms of contractual savings.

The insurance industry in Ireland can trace its origins to the early eighteenth century. It has become more competitive since the 1960s, partly as a result of acquisitions of a number of medium-sized Irish firms by foreign companies as well as significant additional entry into Ireland of such companies. About 20 per cent of insurance premium income now accrues to Irish-owned insurance firms, while about 55 per cent of assurance premium income flows to the Irish-owned assurance companies. A feature of the insurance industry is that insurance policies can only be sold by a firm that has a commercial presence in Ireland and is licensed by the Irish authorities. Improvements in the quality and variety of assurance and insurance products in recent years have also helped to make the industry more competitive.

The insurance industry in Ireland has recorded a more rapid rate of growth since the mid-1970s than that experienced in a number of countries in the EC where, in contrast to banking and securities activities, the insurance industry has been protected from the full force of international competition. The higher rate of growth that occurred in Ireland was accompanied by major prudential problems in the 1980s in two Irish-owned insurance firms which, between them, accounted for about one-fifth of the domestic insurance market.

Prudential difficulties have been experienced in the insurance industry from time to time over the past fifty years. In 1938, four small assurance companies (City of Dublin Assurance Company, Irish Life and General Assurance Company, Irish National Assurance Company and Munster and Leinster Assurance Company) revealed deficiencies in their assets relative to their liabilities. These amounted to £1 million in aggregate (equivalent to some £30 million today) and were made good by the Minister for Finance.

The Equitable Insurance Company was wound up in 1963, while the Private Motorists Protection

GILTS
Government securities, bonds or stocks that are issued by the government in exchange for funds borrowed. They yield interest each year to those who hold or own them.

EQUITIES
Shares issued by limited companies for the purposes of raising capital. The owner of the equities or shares is paid a dividend out of profits earned by the company.

Association (PMPA) was temporarily placed under Administration by the government in 1983 with a view to protecting policy-holders and arranging for the gradual elimination of the deficiencies that had arisen. Six years later, in 1989, the viable ongoing business of PMPA was sold to Guardian Royal Exchange. In 1985, Allied Irish Bank wrote off nearly one quarter of its capital base at that time when its wholly-owned insurance subsidiary — The Insurance Corporation of Ireland plc — experienced substantial losses and was also placed, and continues, under Administration. The Insurance Compensation Fund was established in 1964 for the purpose of meeting certain liabilities of insurance companies that experience prudential difficulties.

Since the 1960s, deficiencies that occur in the assets of insurance companies are gradually financed by annual contributions borne directly by the private sector, rather than by the authorities as occurred in 1938. Steps were taken in the 1989 Insurance Act to exclude corporate and externally issued policies from falling within the scope of any protection that may be provided in the future under the Insurance Compensation Fund. All of the customer-compensation arrangements now in place in the financial sector (whether in respect of depositors with banks, building societies and credit unions, holders of insurance policies and clients of stockbroking firms, but not assurance policies in respect of which there are no specific compensation arrangements) are limited to providing comfort to the personal customers of these institutions, a policy which is in line with international practice.

Generous fiscal incentives have favoured savings with life assurance companies at the expense of savings with banks, other deposit-taking institutions and direct personal holdings of gilts and equities. The state has also promoted a major assurance company — Irish Life Assurance plc. This company was founded by the state some fifty years ago (by amalgamating, in 1939, the four Irish-owned life companies and the Irish business of five British life offices) and has built up a market share not far short of 50 per cent of the life assurance market in Ireland. Irish Life Assurance has also been expanding abroad since the mid-1960s. It established its first area office in the UK in 1967 and by the late 1980s was deriving one-third of its individual business annual premium income from there. In 1988, it acquired Inter-State Assurance Company, Iowa — a firm that can write business throughout most of the American states. Consideration is being given by the authorities to the nature of the appropriate capital and ownership structure of Irish Life Assurance for the future.

Ownership inter-linkages exist between assurance and banking, in the sense that Irish Life Assurance holds a substantial interest (in the range of 10 to 15 per cent) of the issued share capital of both Allied Irish Bank and Bank of Ireland. Irish Life Assurance also has a 25 per cent holding in Irish Intercontinental Bank. As regards banks owning assurance companies, Bank of Ireland established a wholly owned life assurance subsidiary in 1987, while Allied Irish Bank has applied for authorisation to enter the life assurance business. Banks are discouraged from owning general insurance firms as distinct from assurance companies and, at this stage, no bank owns an insurance company nor is there a case of a bank being fully or substantially owned by an insurance company. The marketing of insurance products and the ownership of insurance broking firms or agencies by banks is not discouraged since, in such circumstances, banks are primarily involved on an agency basis and not in a principal capacity (which would entail onerous responsibilities).

Over the past two decades, but especially in the 1980s, the life assurance companies, both Irish-owned and foreign, have been playing an increasing role in the overall domestic savings market and now account for about half of it. While the protective, longer term assurance products are not close substitutes for deposits with banks, building societies and other deposit-taking institutions, the shorter term and reasonably liquid savings-oriented assurance products may be regarded as close substitutes for deposits, as well as for diversified personal portfolios of gilts, equities and other investments. On offer in recent years were guaranteed income and growth bonds, investment bonds without guaranteed performance, and single premium and more conventional regular premium savings policies — all supported by life assurance cover. These products have provided competition for medium-sized savings in banks and building societies, and also for direct personal holdings of equities and gilts.

Following the 1986 and subsequent Budgets, some of these facilities have become less attractive, especially guaranteed income and growth bonds. With a further movement towards a more equal tax treatment of all financial institutions, the entry of banks into life assurance and the marketing of assurance products by deposit-taking institutions and some bank products by assurance companies, competition in the 1990s between the domestic deposit-taking financial institutions and the assurance companies will take place on a more level basis than in the 1980s. In the 1990s, the assurance industry will be concentrating on competition arising from within the domestic assurance industry itself and also on the implications of EC directives for European-wide competition within the industry. It may be less concerned with direct competition from the other domestic financial institutions and personal portfolios of gilts and equities than it was in the 1980s. A number of EC directives will gradually come into force over the 1990s which will allow a company to sell its products more freely across national boundaries without having to have a commercial presence there or to be licensed by the authorities of the country concerned. A cooperative agreement entered into in mid-1989 among nine European assurance companies (including Irish Life Assurance), to establish a network between them for sharing and exchanging information and products, may be a tentative move in this direction.

SECURITIES INDUSTRY

There have been significant changes since the 1960s in the structures of both the stock exchanges in Ireland and their member firms which, in broad terms, may be described as the securities industry. There has always been close cooperation between the exchanges in Ireland and those in Britain. The Irish exchanges derived significant benefits (in the form of information, advice and technical services) down the years from participating in these international stock exchange arrangements. A loose agreement between the exchanges of Ireland and Britain emerged in 1965, when the Federation of Stock Exchanges in Great Britain and Ireland was established. This helped to achieve uniform minimum standards in relation to such matters as the issuing and publication of prices for securities and qualifications of stock exchange members. It also allowed member-firms of the exchanges to participate in a central client compensation fund that could be drawn upon in the event of the failure of

The market floor of the Irish Stock Exchange. Trading began in 1793 when a voluntary association of stockbrokers was formed. In 1986, the Irish Stock Exchange became part of the International Stock Exchange of the United Kingdom and the Republic of Ireland

a stockbroking firm, of which there has been two such experiences in recent decades.

Steps towards consolidation within the Republic were taken in the late 1960s and, in March 1971, all of the exchanges in the Republic (Dublin, Cork and other areas) came together to establish the Irish Stock Exchange. Within two years, the exchanges in Ireland and Britain were formally amalgamated in 1973 under the title The Stock Exchange, with the exchanges in the Republic and Belfast being recognised as the Irish Unit and the Belfast Unit, respectively, of the London-based exchange.

From the mid-1970s onwards, major advances in communications technology occurred, at the same time as the removal of barriers to capital movements internationally, more intense international competition and lower computing costs in the securities industry. This resulted in a major reorganisation — known as 'Big Bang' — of the securities industry in London in the mid-1980s. Arising from these international developments, the Irish Stock Exchange became part of the International Stock Exchange of the United Kingdom and the Republic of Ireland in 1986. This arrangement enables the Irish Stock Exchange to participate in a highly developed computerised system for quoting, clearing and settling securities transactions.

However, one of the results of these changes in the mid-1980s is that there has been some weakening of the Irish connection with London, since the large central compensation fund no longer brings comfort to the Irish clients of stockbroking firms in Ireland. A new insurance-based fund has recently been established, extending to Ireland, the Isle of Man and the Channel Islands; its purpose is to provide cover to the personal clients of stockbroking firms in these areas. A further weakening of the relationship with London may arise as the supervision of the Irish Stock Exchange and its local member-firms is localised before the coming into effect of the draft EC Investment Services Directive by the end of 1992. The

THE IRISH STOCK EXCHANGE
A market, situated in Dublin, where gilts and equities are purchased and sold, and where capital is raised on behalf of companies and the government.

application of appropriate best practices to determining the prices of gilts and equities in the Dublin markets could also lead to a further loosening of the connection with London.

Apart from the amalgamation of the exchanges in Ireland since the mid-1960s and their closer association with what has been occurring in the securities industry internationally, there has been increasing concentration among the Irish stockbroking firms themselves. Prior to the mid-1970s, over half the stock exchange firms consisted of two partners. The number of such firms has fallen markedly since then, with six multipartner firms now conducting most of the business of the stock exchange. This consolidation has been accompanied by major changes in the ownership of stockbroking firms since the mid-1980s. Since banks are no longer prohibited from owning or participating in stockbroking firms, a number of such firms in the Republic are now associated with or owned by banks.

MARKET-MAKING
This describes the state of being in constant readiness to buy or sell a security in reasonable amounts and at bid and offer prices attractive enough to encourage purchases and sales of the security concerned. Market-making helps to improve liquidity, increase turnover and disseminate changes in prices.

With regard to gilts transactions, the stockbroking firms are confined to acting as agents for their customers, with minimum commissions stipulated by the authorities. An implication of these arrangements is that there are no firms engaged in market-making in Irish gilts. In the case of equities, negotiable commissions are applicable and the stockbroking firms may act in a dual capacity, that is, acquire or sell equities on their own account, as well as acting as agents for their customers. In acting on their own account or in a principal capacity, they would contribute to the marketability of the equities concerned. So far, the market-making function is not a developed feature of the equity market in Ireland.

The market for government securities, which accounts for nearly 90 per cent of the overall turnover on the stock exchange, has increased enormously since the 1960s because of the very large amount of government borrowing since then. The market in equities has remained limited despite the revived interest since 1983. With the ready availability of high-yielding gilts, there was little pressure to increase the supply of equities and introduce marketable securities for financing investment in property. But, with the introduction of less well-established and smaller companies since 1986, a greater range and amount of Irish equities will be coming available in the decade ahead, despite the increased uncertainty of the equity market since October 1987. The equity market is now growing more rapidly than the gilt or government bond market.

Government borrowing is increasing more slowly than in the past as the excess of government expenditure over tax revenue is getting smaller. Companies, however, are raising an increasing amount of funds by issuing shares because, in recent years, it has become more attractive to raise funds in this relatively liberal manner rather than relying on the more confining conventional sources, particularly bank credit. Companies are also having increasing resort to the emerging commercial paper market in Dublin, which, however, is outside the influence of the Irish Stock Exchange. This market is now more clearly defined and poised for further development following the guidelines issued recently by the Central Bank about raising funds in the form of commercial paper.

International business conducted on the Irish Stock Exchange is increasing relative to domestic business. Foreign investors are acquiring Irish securities, especially government bonds. Irish savers are also availing themselves of the opportunity once again, following the liberalisation of exchange controls in 1988 and 1989, to diversify their portfolios by increasing their holdings of foreign securities.

The channelling of funds from savers to companies and the public sector by the issue of securities on the stock exchange is not a serious competitive challenge for the banks. This is because the main Irish holders of government securities (excluding the banks themselves) are the building societies, insurance companies and pension funds.

These institutions compete directly with the banks
for the savings of their personal customers, whose
direct holdings of gilts are declining in importance.
This is because of tax incentives and cost advantages
that nowadays tend to favour the institutional rather
than the personal management of funds and
portfolios.

Nor is the issue of equities a serious threat to the
banks because so far the total amount of funds raised
by issues of equities (excluding those issued by the
banks themselves) is not substantial and also because
the amount of equities directly held by potential
bank depositors is relatively small. In addition, it
must be recognised that the banks probably
welcome the lowering of the risk in their lending
portfolio owing to the improvement in the
capitalisation of Irish companies (which also raise
funds by borrowing from the banks). Finally, the
impact on the banks of a major reduction in the
market for channelling funds via the banks from
savers to borrowers, as a result of a relatively
substantial increase in the amount of equities issued,
would be cushioned by the fact that the banks now
own, or can acquire, stockbroking or security firms.

EXTENDING ABROAD

At the same time as foreign banks were creating a
more competitive domestic banking environment,
the two major Irish banking groups — Allied Irish
Bank and Bank of Ireland — were gaining
experience in expanding abroad. This is now
reflected in the expected contribution, of the order
of 50 per cent, to their profits from earnings outside
the country. This increase in the international
activities of Irish banks is additional to, and not to
be confused with, the relatively rapid growth in
their international banking business with non-
residents that is conducted from offices located
within the state, including the International
Financial Services Centre.

Leaving aside for the moment their presence in Northern Ireland, both groups established a foothold in the British retail banking sector in the 1970s, where their branch network increased from a few branches in 1970 to thirty in 1975 and to some sixty in 1989. The Bank of Ireland group entered into instalment-credit banking in the UK in 1978 by acquiring a small local bank and, in 1987, acquired another bank that specialises in mortgage finance. At this stage, the Irish banks have a larger share of retail banking in Britain than the other external banks who have directly established themselves there in local retail banking.

In 1988, Bank of Ireland acquired a regional banking group in New Hampshire, USA. Allied Irish Bank had already entered domestic banking in the United States in 1983 through the purchase of a major share in a medium-sized regional bank in Maryland; it acquired full ownership of it in March 1989. The two groups have also established themselves in the City of London and, since the mid-1970s, in New York and environs; more recently, they have moved into the international financial centres of Singapore, Hong Kong and Sydney. In addition to these locations, both banks are represented in Brussels, Frankfurt, Jersey, Isle of Man, Cayman Islands, Chicago and Tokyo. One of the smaller Irish banks — Anglo-Irish Bank Corporation — is also involved in instalment-credit and leasing in the UK, where it has a local presence.

NORTHERN IRELAND: CHANGES IN BANKING STRUCTURE

During the 1960s, there were significant mergers between the banks in Northern Ireland. The third and last of the clearing banks centred on Belfast was merged into the British clearing bank system when the Midland Bank took over the Northern Banking Company in 1965 and proceeded to integrate the Belfast Banking Company with it by 1970.

Subsequently, in 1986, the Midland Bank established separate subsidiaries for the Republic and the Northern Ireland business of the Northern Bank and, in 1987, sold both subsidiaries to the major retail-oriented National Australia Bank.

The Ulster Bank had been a subsidiary of a UK clearing bank since 1917. It became part of a wider clearing group — National Westminster Group — in 1968 with the amalgamation of its parent with another UK clearing bank. During the 1930s and 1940s, all the savings banks in Northern Ireland (except the Enniskillen Savings Bank) merged with the Belfast Savings Bank. In 1974, the Enniskillen and Belfast savings banks were merged to form the Trustee Savings Bank of Northern Ireland, which changed its name once again in 1986 to TSB Northern Ireland plc, when it became a fully owned subsidiary with full banking status of the London-based and recently privatised Trustee Savings Bank (Holdings) Limited. There were thirteen British-based building societies in operation in Northern Ireland in 1988, compared with only two small locally registered societies. It is noteworthy that since the mid-1960s no major private financial institution operating in Northern Ireland (whether bank, building society or insurance company) was locally owned.

The structural changes in banking in Northern Ireland followed a similar pattern to those occurring in the Republic. Industrial or instalment-credit banking subsidiaries were established by the Northern Ireland clearing banks in the 1960s, to compete mainly with the branches and subsidiaries of British industrial banks, some of which in turn were subsidiaries of British clearing banks that did not have clearing bank subsidiaries in Northern Ireland. Merchant banking subsidiaries were also established by the Northern Ireland clearing banks, partly to avoid paying relatively high rates of interest across the board on deposits at their retail branches. A limited number of US banks also opened branches in Belfast in the early 1970s, but they subsequently withdrew. Apart from the actions of their subsidiary clearing banks in Northern Ireland, British banks did not directly establish merchant bank subsidiaries there.

The indications are that clearing banking business relative to other forms of banking activities are larger in Northern Ireland than in the Republic. This partly reflects the relatively large foreign bank presence and significant non-resident business of the subsidiaries of the clearing banks in the Republic, and also the extent to which business firms in Northern Ireland have resort externally, especially for non-clearing banking and related services. Another interesting feature of Northern Ireland is that the per capita value of the currency notes in circulation seems to be much higher than in the Republic.

Building societies and insurance companies, which played a larger role in Northern Ireland than in the Republic in the earlier decades of this century, continued to develop in Northern Ireland over the past twenty years along similar lines to those in the Republic. The number of building society branches in Northern Ireland rose from 28 in 1975 to 104 in 1988. Nowadays, savings with building societies are about half as large as those with the clearing banks, a similar situation to that in the Republic. The National Savings Bank and the National Girobank (like the Post Office Savings Bank in the Republic) have not retained their market shares, which in aggregate have fallen to around 2 per cent. The TSB Northern Ireland has had the opportunity, since the mid-1970s, to move steadily towards privatisation with the substitution of private lending for holdings of government securities. This development is evolving much more slowly in the Republic, where the role played by the trustee savings banks is smaller than in Northern Ireland.

The indications are that competition between credit institutions in Northern Ireland, especially for retail business, will continue to increase. This is because of the enlarged scope for the extension of services provided by building societies under the 1986 UK building societies legislation, the greater thrust behind the TSB since privatisation and the probable introduction by the clearing banks of interest on current accounts. Each of the clearing banks in Northern Ireland has set its own levels of interest rates since January 1985, when the joint setting of interest rates was discontinued.

One of the main differences between the Republic and the Northern Ireland financial sectors is that locally oriented financial markets did not evolve to any significant extent in Northern Ireland. Given the pattern of external receipts and payments of the Northern Ireland economy, it is probable that the passive nature of the financial markets in Northern Ireland has led to sizeable holdings of assets outside Northern Ireland by Northern Ireland residents. Other distinctive, but related features of Northern Ireland are that it is not bearing a high per capita level of marketable public debt, especially vis-à-vis non-residents of Northern Ireland, and that it does not have an independent currency.

These features partly account for the absence of indigenous capital, money and foreign exchange markets in Northern Ireland. Broadly speaking, the banking system in Northern Ireland continues to be relatively retail and local in orientation and to centre its liquidity requirements on London, since it is fully integrated into the UK financial system. This leads to outflows and the importation of financial market services by the financial institutions. The non-bank residents of Northern Ireland probably spread their holdings of external assets more widely than residents of the Republic, in the form of claims on Britain, the Republic, the Isle of Man and other offshore centres.

STRATEGIC AIMS

Irish banking has evolved over the past twenty-five years from relatively passive membership of the sterling area banking system with its liquidity centred on London. In the 1960s, it took its first major initiative in this century when it pursued the defensive strategy of consolidating domestically. This facilitated the spreading of overheads, the automation of back-office processing and the introduction of centralised managerial control. As a result, the banks were strengthened to face strong competition at home from foreign banks and from non-bank domestic financial institutions that were the beneficiaries of relatively favourable taxation arrangements, at the same time establishing a sound domestic base from which to extend abroad. Employment in banking and related services in the 1980s accounts for nearly 3 per cent of total employment, compared with less than 1 per cent in the 1960s. It is estimated that in the late 1980s there were at least 22,000 employed in banks, compared with nearly 2,000 in building societies, some 9,000 in insurance companies and somewhat over 500 in stockbroking firms.

A more competitive climate between the major Irish banks themselves has been emerging since the mid-1980s, with their greater scope for setting interest rates independently, their more rigorous pursuit of a group-oriented business strategy and their enhanced commitment to customer service. These developments are eroding the distinctions between their clearing, merchant and industrial banking activities, as promoted in the 1960s, and integrating more closely the overall control of their retail, corporate, treasury and overseas activities.

Since 1983, the banks have been pursuing their second major domestic initiative in this century — to maintain and increase their share of the overall domestic market by bringing banking to the customer. On this occasion, the emphasis is on producing a wider range of higher value products, applying computerised technology to delivering them to customers and decentralising certain decision-making responsibilities. These changes are leading to a shift of emphasis from back-office production of services to front-office sales and product development, and are posing major challenges for manpower planning, training and technological investment.

Alongside these domestic developments in the clearing banks, a number of changes have been occurring among the other banks in the Republic, involving ownership, pruning of branches and other structural adjustments. These changes are being introduced with a view to providing additional products, applying up-to-date technology and minimising overhead and manpower costs.

The banks are responding to the growing competition between financial institutions by extending in a number of directions. They are becoming directly involved in stockbroking firms and to a limited extent underwriting issues of securities as the boundaries between banking and stockbroking or securities activities are eroding. Banks are also becoming much more involved, in a fiduciary capacity, in managing portfolios for pension funds, trusts, charities and private clients, and in the marketing and management of collective investments such as unit trusts. Furthermore, they are also establishing assurance subsidiaries and marketing insurance products on an agency basis. The wide range of non-banking activities nowadays undertaken by banks will probably grow in relative importance in the future as barriers are lowered between different types of financial institutions. This may result in banks becoming major financial supermarkets in their efforts to increase their share of the overall market for savings and financial services.

The extent to which banks will establish themselves as financial supermarkets in the future will depend to a certain extent on the behaviour of their customers. Customers may be concerned that where a bank's interests and those of its customers conflict, the bank may operate against the customers. Moreover, customers may not wish to lose contact with a wide range of independent financial institutions. These concerns would be mitigated by a number of factors, such as greater competition between financial supermarkets; separate incorporation within the supermarkets of specialist financial services; strict barriers to the

FIDUCIARY CAPACITY
The business a bank conducts on behalf of a customer when it acts as an agent rather than as a principal. This term also indicates that a person or institution is acting as trustee for another.

exchange of confidential information about customers between the different areas of business conducted by the financial supermarkets; enhanced arrangements for investigating customer grievances; and the introduction of an agreed code of conduct for advertising and marketing financial products by all the financial institutions engaged in the provision of financial services to personal customers.

As well as consolidating in the 1960s and diversifying in the 1980s, the banks have also been expanding abroad, especially since the early 1980s. They have established a significant presence internationally relative to their domestic activities. With the emergence of the single financial market throughout Europe in the decade ahead, all banks, and indeed all other financial institutions, now operating in Ireland must remain internationally competitive. This will call for a reduction in the relatively high interest and expense margins that exist in Irish banking and an improvement in the quality of their products required by their customers. Otherwise their shares of the Irish and European banking markets will decline — a development that would have a greater impact on the banks themselves than on some of their customers, who will have access in the years ahead to a wider range of external financial institutions.

Past experiences with international competition, and with takeovers and mergers, would suggest that competition that is not excessively aggressive and is conducted in an orderly manner tends to be beneficial to both bank shareholders, bank staff and bank customers. Over time, competition and the threat of being taken over improves operational efficiency and leads to the introduction of innovations which provide customers with the international range of services they demand at competitive prices.

It remains to be seen what will be the ultimate implications of international competition, greater customer choice and the overall integration of financial markets, including the realisation of the single European market, for the future structure of

*FINANCIAL
INTEGRATION
The process whereby the
financial sectors
(excluding the monetary
authorities) of different
economies become
interlinked across
national boundaries as a
result of strong
competition, improved
communications and
harmonised supervisory
and taxation systems.
Financial integration is
advancing rapidly in
Europe as a result of
the commitment to
establish the single
financial market. It is
also underway between
the USA, Japan and
Europe and, indeed,
between Ireland and
other countries.*

Irish banking, both in Ireland and abroad. We can be confident, however, that the strategic objectives of the dynamic and growing companies in the financial sector will continue to change and that their organisational structures, management capacity and global control systems will continue to evolve, in order to ensure success in the rapidly changing international financial services industry. Whether financial institutions located in Ireland orient themselves towards the regional or specialised segments of the European financial sector, it would seem appropriate, in the context of EC regional development policy, that they be encouraged by, for example, the development of the International Financial Services Centre to arrange their affairs so as to maximise the proportion of their value added that is located in and flows to Ireland.

In addition to these structural developments in recent decades, Irish banking also had to accommodate itself to significant changes in the role of the Central Bank.

CENTRAL BANKING: COMING OF AGE

It was recognised at the time the Central Bank was established in the early 1940s that confidence in the currency would not be maintained if central banking was confined solely to managing the issue and redemption of notes and coins and to ensuring that those in circulation were fully supported by external assets. Thus, from the early 1950s onwards, the Central Bank found it necessary to express concern publicly about increases in public expenditure and bank credit that did not seem consistent over time with maintaining the value or purchasing power of the currency. It has continued to do so in subsequent decades against the background of a much deeper analysis of the causes of monetary instability and with varying degrees of emphasis, depending on the seriousness of the emerging monetary trends and their balance of payments implications.

MONETARY POLICY
The policy formulated and implemented by the Central Bank to stabilise the value of the currency on the international foreign exchange markets and to minimise general increases in domestic prices. Monetary policy is implemented by focusing on the magnitude of the banks' domestic liquid assets and the differences between the levels of interest rates in Ireland and abroad, with a view to maintaining adequate reserves of foreign currencies and influencing domestic credit conditions.

The Central Bank has also been developing over the years its techniques and methods for the purposes of implementing its monetary policy objectives. While monetary policy has always had the objective of minimising inflation, the manner in which this objective has been articulated and conveyed, and the means used to realise or attain it have been continuously evolving.

It was the emergence of difficulties in the balance of payments in the mid-1950s that required the Central Bank to take its first steps in developing the techniques for implementing monetary policy. The Central Bank responded positively at the time to requests from the clearing banks to provide them with temporary accommodation during a sharp contraction in their foreign liquid assets. Prior to the mid-1950s, adverse developments in the balance of payments did not impinge on the adequacy of the banks' liquidity or encashable assets, which was

Foster Place in Dublin, from a sketch by Sean Keating, was the premises of the Central Bank until 1969, when the bank's main business was moved to Fitzwilton House, awaiting the building of new offices in Dame Street. Foster Place was originally acquired in 1928 by the Currency Commission, forerunner of the Central Bank, from the Bank of Ireland

CURRENT ACCOUNT
A customer's account with a bank on which cheques are drawn and into which funds are paid or lodged in a variety of forms — coins, notes, cheques. The account usually bears no direct interest on credit balances, although competition between banks is eroding this tradition.

DEPOSIT ACCOUNT
An interest-bearing credit balance with a bank, which may be withdrawn on demand or after a specified time, depending on the precise features of the account. There is a wide variety of such accounts.

at a comfortable level due mainly to the trade surpluses of earlier decades.

There was also a reluctance in the 1950s and in subsequent decades to allow Irish interest rates to rise in line with those abroad, which had been increasing from the artificially low levels set at the beginning of World War II. This attitude towards rising interest rates was accompanied by increasing government outlays for capital purposes which, at times, it was difficult to finance by borrowing from domestic sources other than banks. The need for the banks to hold foreign or external assets continued to be questioned in the 1950s, as it had been since the 1920s, without reference to the rate of return that they might earn if they were invested domestically. Furthermore, the banks' domestic lending was increasing at an unsustainable rate. These were the main features of the financial scene in Ireland around the mid-1950s.

RELYING ON CREDIT GUIDELINES

It is not surprising that balance of payments problems emerged in the mid-1950s. The Central Bank played a major role in exposing the main causes of the difficulties, especially the unsustainable increase in bank credit that led to temporary borrowing by the banks from the Central Bank to meet their shortages of liquidity abroad. These experiences were accompanied by a sharp tightening of fiscal policy, with the Central Bank embarking on a more significant role than formerly in discussions and consultations concerning the responsibility of the banking system in financial and economic policy. A liquidity standard for the banks was subsequently introduced in 1958. This specified a minimum level of external assets and balances at the Central Bank relative to their domestic resources (that is, their current and deposit accounts).

Balance of payments difficulties developed again in the mid-1960s for a number of reasons. This led

OFFICIAL EXTERNAL
RESERVES
*The external assets or
reserves held by the
Central Bank to bridge
temporarily the gaps
that arise when the
country's payments
abroad exceed its foreign
receipts. Confidence in
the exchange rate is
maintained by having
adequate official
external reserves, which
are the last line of
defence in meeting
excess external
payments.*

to a deepening of the influence of the Central Bank over the rate of increase in domestic bank lending. While the Central Bank had been relying on the voluntary cooperation of the clearing banks in managing their liquid assets relative to the movements in their domestic resources, it decided to strengthen its hand in the summer of 1965 at a time of contraction in the official external reserves.

This followed a request from the clearing banks, in the light of the deterioration in their liquidity, for advice about the appropriate magnitude of the future growth in their credit. In the context of coming to grips with the external payments difficulties, the Central Bank took the opportunity to advise the banks about the appropriate magnitude of future increases in their domestic lending that exceeded the growth in their deposit resources (excluding that in the form of credit balances on current accounts). The Central Bank also embarked on consultations with individual banks about their direct contribution to the attainment of the overall credit policy objective.

Changes in interest rates that reflected international developments, as well as quantitative guidelines, were relied upon for the purposes of implementing credit policy for the next twenty years or so, up to the mid-1980s. A debate took place in the late 1960s about the extent to which it was appropriate to continue to regard only the increase in bank lending that was in excess of the growth in domestic deposits as representing additional money arising within the country. Up to then, deposits were not considered as part of the money in circulation, since the emphasis was on the motives for holding money for making payments rather than for the purposes of accumulating wealth, reflecting the state of development of the economy and the emphasis in monetary analysis.

There was a new dimension to this debate towards the end of the 1960s with the growing importance of the newly emerging banks. These recently established banks were not only attracting some of the newly accumulated savings, but were also diverting existing deposits away from the long-established clearing banks. It was considered that this competitive process was changing the character of deposits, from representing long-term inactive savings or holdings of wealth to being closer to money held for transactions purposes as represented by the credit balances on current account.

In the light of these developments, it was decided at the end of the 1960s to direct the Central Bank's credit advice towards the gross or total annual increase in lending by all banks. Quantitative limits were also placed on inflows from abroad through banks, since, in those days, it was considered that they were the main channels for mobile inflows from abroad and it had been feared that such inflows could easily become excessive in the lax international monetary climate that prevailed.

The quantitative credit guidelines on inflows had to be supported during the early 1970s with arrangements for the placing by banks of relatively low interest-bearing balances at the Central Bank to discourage excess inflows of funds from abroad through banks. Penal rates of interest for excessive borrowing from the Central Bank also had to be applied. Rising international inflation, floating exchange rates, the oil crisis of 1973 and, of course, the growing domestic current budget deficits from 1972 onwards brought about the application of these specific measures with a view to limiting the growth in domestic bank lending.

A major shift of emphasis was required in 1978. The economy had moved rapidly towards domestic inflation of the order of 20 per cent, unsustainable external and budgetary imbalances of over 15 per cent of GNP and inordinate annual rates of increase of over 30 per cent in domestic bank credit. Additional penalties on banks had to be introduced in the form of relatively low interest-bearing balances at the Central Bank, equal to the excess of lending over that advised, in order to give banks an incentive not to exceed the quantitative limits placed on their lendings.

The changes over the decades in the orientation

and approaches to implementing monetary policy partly reflected the structural changes that were occurring in the banking system. They also reflected the inordinate magnitude of additional money that was being placed in circulation by government borrowing and the shifts in the orientation of monetary and financial analyses to take account of the changes in emphasis and the findings of monetary research.

MONETARY INTEGRATION
In Europe, this is the ultimate stage of active coordination of monetary policy between member-countries. Monetary integration is concerned with realising greater stability between exchange rates, minimising inflation and eventually leading to a single currency area and full monetary union. A route to monetary integration within the EC has been mapped out in the Delors Committee Report, published in 1989.

Despite the anti-competitive nature of such guidelines, they had to be rigorously applied up to the mid-1980s, by which time the price of oil and the international and domestic rates of inflation were substantially lower, the balance of payments deficit was significantly reduced and the rate of increase in bank lending was no longer a threat to stable monetary conditions. Since then, the direct approach of using credit ceilings for the purposes of implementing credit policy has been placed in suspension and, currently, the Central Bank is relying on indirect methods in implementing monetary policy, that is, on the management of the movements in external reserves, bank liquidity and interest rates.

This shift in focus partly reflects the international diversification of portfolios and the growing mobility of capital, not only across frontiers but between different domestic financial institutions as well. It also reflects the more widespread appreciation that the efficient control of movements of funds is through timely variations in the prices at which financial assets are traded or exchanged. However, the effectiveness of full reliance on the indirect approach to the implementation of monetary policy, both in Ireland and in a number of other countries, has not been fully tested in such highly inflationary circumstances as prevailed from the late 1960s to the early 1980s. It will be of interest to see how credit will be controlled as monetary integration progresses in Europe.

LOCALISING BANK LIQUIDITY

At the same time as direct quantitative measures were being applied, the Central Bank had also been developing its capacity to influence bank lending indirectly. The indirect approach evolved more slowly than the direct quantitative methods, since it depended on the rate of development of the domestic financial markets. The Central Bank gave its full support to this over the years, including the establishment of a committee of inquiry in 1967 to advise on future developments in the money market. The change of emphasis in the 1980s reflects the innovations that have been made in Irish financial markets since the mid-1960s, but especially since the decision to join the EMS in the late 1970s.

The first indirect steps taken by the Central Bank to manage bank liquidity occurred in the mid-1950s, when it temporarily accepted domestic paper from the banks and supplied them in turn with external balances that were used to meet their adverse clearings of cheques abroad. This was followed in 1958 by the first positive approach by the banks to building up domestic liquidity when they agreed to maintain their domestic cheque-clearing accounts at the Central Bank rather than retaining balances in London for this purpose.

Another move in this direction occurred in 1964, when the Central Bank was empowered to pay interest on deposits that the banks themselves placed with the Central Bank; this resulted in a further addition to the level of balances that the banks retained at the Central Bank. Exchequer financing problems and balance of payments difficulties in 1965/66 resulted in the Central Bank providing a relatively large level of temporary accommodation to the clearing banks, at the same time as credit guidelines were being tightened and Exchequer borrowing (from the Central Bank, the International Monetary Fund and the external capital markets) was being embarked upon to finance public capital expenditure. The combination of these steps helped to prevent a serious reduction in the level of domestic bank liquidity, which was being built up slowly since 1958.

In 1967, about one-third of the external monetary reserves of the country, or somewhat over one-fifth of the banks' domestic current and deposit accounts, continued to be held by the clearing banks in the form of foreign liquid assets. However, the centralisation of bank liquidity at the Central Bank advanced rapidly in 1968 and 1969, with the lead being given by the Central Bank itself. This occurred in the wake of the 1967 devaluation of sterling and the concerns about inflation in the UK, the recognition internationally that the days of the sterling area were numbered and the accompanying steps to diversify the sterling external reserves by transferring them to the Central Bank for investment in a wider range of currencies. The centralisation of bank liquidity also occurred against a domestic background in which the banks were taking up tranches of government paper annually which were not marketable.

As a result of these developments, the role of the Central Bank in the management of bank liquidity was rapidly extended, especially in 1969 when the Bank arranged for the transfer to it of the remaining external reserves of the banks and simultaneously provided a wide range of short-term deposit facilities for banks. Thus, by the end of the 1960s, the management of bank liquidity had been switched from London, where it had been centred for at least the previous 150 years, to Dublin, where money and gilt markets were evolving. The conversion of the banks' sterling liquid assets into Irish-pound denominated liquidity in the second half of the 1960s prepared the way for the break in the link with sterling in 1979. This was achieved by the virtual elimination of a major mismatch between assets and liabilities expressed in sterling that, at least in strict legal terms, had existed in Irish banking since the late 1920s. This first occurred when the banks' domestic liabilities and assets were expressed in Irish pounds, at the same time as their external liabilities and assets remained expressed in sterling. Down the years, confidence in the sterling link, together with the view that the Irish pound would devalue against sterling if the link were broken, eliminated concerns about the sterling net asset position of the banks.

DEVELOPING FINANCIAL MARKETS

The main events in the Irish gilt market in the decade prior to the 1970s were the issue of the annual national loan for public subscription and the occasional negotiations initiated by the government with the clearing banks for the uptake by the banks of an issue of government securities. Such negotiations became more frequent in the second half of the 1960s with the growth in public capital expenditure. In those days, gilts were mainly held to maturity rather than switched or traded to any significant degree, since the proportion of gilts or bonds held by institutions and non-residents was relatively low. It was against this background that the Central Bank began to take steps to develop the domestic financial markets, at the same time as private initiatives were leading to the emergence of the inter-bank market in Irish pounds.

EXCHEQUER BILL
A bill issued by the Irish Exchequer in respect of money borrowed, usually for three months. It promises to pay the holder a specific sum of money when it is redeemed.

The Exchequer Bill market was improved from 1969 onwards, when the Central Bank assumed responsibility for the monthly issue of bills to the clearing banks and subsequently drew the recently established banks and other domestic financial institutions into the Exchequer Bill market. A weekly tender for Exchequer Bills was subsequently introduced in 1980 and nowadays the Central Bank stands ready to buy and sell outstanding Exchequer Bills at prices that reflect current money market interest rates. Improvements in the variety, availability and marketability of government paper were gradually introduced in the 1970s; these embraced short, medium and long-dated gilts, with both fixed and variable rates of interest. In the

*PRIMARY AND
SECONDARY MARKETS
New issues of securities
are launched
on the 'primary'
market; subsequent sales
and purchases are
conducted on the
'secondary' market.
Transactions in
marketable securities
(other than those
associated with the
issuing or redemption of
them) are described as
secondary market
transactions.*

1980s, there have been further improvements in the depth and liquidity of the domestic gilt market, with increasing turnover and rapid growth in the secondary gilt market, especially since the mid-1980s.

Liquidity ratios were formally established in 1972 and consolidated the substitution that had already occurred, of domestic for foreign liquid assets, by requiring all banks to hold a specified proportion of their current and deposit accounts in balances at the Central Bank and in Irish government paper. The ratios were reduced in 1979, following the impact of the inordinate and unsustainable increase in domestic bank lending in the late 1970s, and the accompanying large build-up of indebtedness by the clearing banks to the Central Bank, which could not have been reversed without a major contraction in the level of bank lending.

No changes have been made since 1979 in the liquidity ratios, which continue to underpin the banks' domestic liquidity. However, the appropriateness of the arrangements is being increasingly questioned against the background of the changes in the 1980s in the domestic financial markets, the methods used for managing bank liquidity and the need for a similar approach to liquidity ratios throughout Europe. No reference, however, is being made in the debate to the common operational needs of monetary policy in Europe and ongoing prudential liquidity requirements.

The Exchequer Account was transferred from the Bank of Ireland to the Central Bank of Ireland on 1 January 1972. Steps were also taken between 1969 and 1974 to transfer the registers of government securities to the Central Bank. In 1974/75, the Central Bank also entered into arrangements to introduce an overdraft facility for the Exchequer to enable it to bridge short-term gaps between Exchequer receipts and expenditure. These changes were also consistent with centralising the management of the banks' liquidity in the Central Bank.

The centralising and diversification of the external reserves also led to the gradual development of the

Dublin foreign exchange market. In 1968, the Central Bank began purchasing surplus foreign currencies (other than sterling) directly from banks and, by 1970, it was also meeting their demands for foreign currencies. With this channelling of the foreign currency business (other than sterling), finer rates of exchange were negotiated. But dealing in foreign currencies between the banks themselves was not being facilitated.

In order to encourage such dealings, the Central Bank took steps in September 1977 to promote inter-bank dealing in foreign currencies. An important outcome of these changes, over the ten years to 1978, was the development of local expertise which facilitated the undertaking of market-making in the Dublin foreign exchange market from 1979 onwards. A market-oriented, forward foreign exchange market for the Irish pound emerged at the same time, following initial support from the Central Bank which, for a short period of time, bore some of the risks involved. The Dublin inter-bank markets in both Irish pounds and foreign currencies, which had been developing throughout the 1970s, also matured in the wake of the break in the fixed link with sterling.

A stage has been reached in Ireland where the

The current £1 note was introduced on 24 November 1977 as part of a series of newly designed notes issued by the Central Bank. It features Medb, legendary Queen of Connaught. It will be replaced by a new £1 coin during 1990

EUROPEAN MONETARY
SYSTEM (EMS)
*This is 'a scheme for
the creation of closer
monetary cooperation,
leading to a zone of
monetary stability in
Europe'. It came into
effect in 1979,
following a Resolution
of the European
Council, and is
establishing a greater
measure of monetary
stability in the EC, as
well as facilitating the
convergence of economic
development. The EMS
is seen as a fundamental
component of a more
comprehensive strategy
aimed at 'lasting growth
with stability, a
progressive return to full
employment, the
harmonisation of living
standards and the
lessening of regional
disparities in the
Community'.*

EXCHANGE RATE
MECHANISM (ERM)
*One of the key features
of the EMS. Most
countries that participate
in the ERM link their
exchange rates to one
another by confining the
fluctuations in them to
plus or minus 2.25 per
cent.*

foreign exchange and domestic money markets are reasonably well developed. Efficient and resilient markets are useful for judging the impact of short-term actions by the Central Bank. Moreover, they help to transmit the medium-term influence of monetary policy throughout the economy, with a view to securing broad price stability over time.

RESPONDING TO THE IMPLICATIONS OF THE EMS

The development of the foreign exchange market occurred under the guidance of the Central Bank, especially in the period following the decision to join the European Monetary System (EMS). Sterling was treated on a par with the other major foreign currencies for the purposes of determining the appropriate magnitude of banks' holdings of foreign exchange and also for the purposes of facilitating the introduction of foreign exchange market-making arrangements. Thus, since the early 1980s, the Dublin foreign exchange market is fully integrated into the international foreign exchange market in the context of membership of the European Exchange Rate Mechanism. It operates within the constraints of the remaining exchange controls on short-term capital movements that were introduced in 1978, when Ireland decided to join the EMS.

The break in the link with sterling also resulted in the introduction of a wide range of techniques by the Central Bank for the purposes of intervening in or influencing the financial markets and managing the liquidity of the banking system. Up to 1979, the daily settlement of banks' residual short-term liquidity continued to be associated with residual transfers of funds to and from London. However, following the break in the link with sterling in March 1979, the Central Bank developed its connection with the domestic money market a stage further, by establishing in July 1979 a residual overnight facility for banks known as the 'short-term facility'. Settlement of banks' money books at the end of each day is now conducted vis-à-vis the Central Bank by variations in the levels of drawings on the short-term facility and in the levels of bankers' overnight balances with the Central Bank.

Other significant innovations in the manner in which the Central Bank provides or withdraws domestic liquidity were to follow in the early 1980s. Arrangements were put in place between the Central Bank and the banks for contracting or expanding domestic liquidity at the initiative of the Central Bank through the use of temporary swaps of foreign currency. Another major innovation was the introduction in 1983 of domestic gilt sale and repurchase arrangements, to be conducted at the initiative of the Central Bank to provide or absorb liquidity through the extension or cancellation of short-term loans to banks.

Membership of the EMS and the break with sterling opened up another chapter in the history of the evolution of the Central Bank. It led to the full integration in the 1980s of what had been happening gradually on three fronts since the late 1960s — namely, the domestic orientation of the management of bank liquidity, the development of the local financial markets and the underpinning of ceilings on bank credit with penalties derived by reference to movements in the local interest rates. In other words, the Central Bank's techniques for influencing or intervening in the foreign-exchange market, as well as in the domestic money market, were developed rapidly following membership of the EMS and, by the mid-1980s, had been fully tested.

PRUDENTIAL SUPERVISION

PRUDENTIAL
SUPERVISION
*The system or
arrangements in place to
ensure that financial
institutions are
adequately capitalised,
managed efficiently and
honestly, and operate so
as to protect
appropriately the
interests of customers
and the stability of the
overall financial system
in a competitive
international
environment.*

The rapid rate of structural change in the banking industry over the past twenty-five years had prudential and risk management implications, which the Central Bank also had to address. In 1965 the Central Bank, in anticipation of the major structural changes in banking in the second half of the 1960s, indicated that it regarded consultation with it as a 'preliminary step in connection with every proposal for the entry of an external institution into banking business in Ireland'. It also made it clear that 'any external bank establishing itself in this country will be expected to show itself responsive to local conditions' and 'to the requirements of public policy in Ireland'.

The Central Bank also endorsed the mergers between the clearing banks in the mid-1960s and expressed 'the hope that they would contribute to a more economic and competitive organisation of Irish commercial banking'. At that time, too, the Central Bank recommended legislation relating to the definition of banking, the licensing of banks and the designation of a bank-licensing authority with discretionary powers. Despite the substantial entry into and significant structural changes in the banking industry since the settled days of the early 1960s, the number of bank failures has been confined to two local institutions of negligible magnitude: one was the Irish Trust Bank Limited, which closed in 1976, and the other, Merchant Banking Limited in 1982.

The legislative proposals recommended by the Central Bank in 1965 were incorporated in the 1971 Central Bank Act and on 1 April 1972, the forty-five existing banks were licensed by the Central Bank. The banks were required to have regard to the provisions and implications of the 1971 Act and to meet various non-statutory standards and requirements set down by the Central Bank. Since then, these standards have been revised and updated on a number of occasions to reflect the changing banking environment, both at home and abroad.

The supervisory role conferred on the Central Bank under the 1971 Act, in the interest of the orderly and proper regulation of banking, has been evolving over the past two decades. It is continuing to do so with the additional wide-ranging legislative support provided by the 1989 Central Bank and Building Societies Acts and the increasing range of EC directives that are, and will be, emerging over the next few years.

Banks and other deposit-taking institutions are unique among financial institutions in the sense that a high proportion of their assets are difficult to assess and value, since they are not marketable, while at the same time all of their liabilities are repayable on demand at predetermined fixed monetary values. In view of this feature of banks and also because they are the main collectors of small savings and administer the cheque-payments systems, the maintenance of public confidence in their ability to meet their liabilities confers significant social benefits on society.

A bank's capacity to meet these responsibilities to society is ultimately related to its overall financial condition, to the quality of its assets and to its capacity to earn profits to remunerate its minimum capital requirements. With this in mind, the Central Bank sets prudential standards for banks. An important objective of these standards is to discourage individual banks from undertaking inappropriate risks by diversifying and avoiding undue concentrations of risk; by holding a specific level of liquid assets; by adequately capitalising themselves; by putting appropriate risk management procedures and controls in place; and by maintaining appropriate management capacity.

The Central Bank collects information from banks to facilitate its monitoring of their adherence to the supervisory standards. It also carries out on-site inspections and, twice yearly, reviews the performance of each bank with its management. Since supervision is not designed to eliminate reasonable risk-bearing, it is appropriate to recall that the ultimate responsibility for preserving the

OFF BALANCE SHEET
ITEMS
Significant contingent
assets and liabilities that
are not included within
the total assets and
liabilities recorded on a
balance sheet. Being 'off
balance sheet' does not
reduce the risks
involved.

EXCHANGE RATE
The price at which a
country's currency can
be exchanged for other
countries' currencies.

soundness and safety of a bank rests with its directors and management.

With the rapid rate of change that is occurring internationally in the structure of banking and in the increased degree of risk to which banks are exposed, major international efforts are being made to raise supervisory standards. The emphasis is on having higher risk-weighted prudential capital standards applied internationally, while at the same time minimising distortions in respect of competition between banks, the location of banking activities and between the different types of business conducted by banks. The standards and practices applied in Ireland continue to evolve in line with best practice in the major industrial countries, particularly in the European Community. Risk-based, capital-adequacy requirements for banks, which are related to a bank's on and off balance sheet assets, have been introduced with effect from early 1990 for banks incorporated in Ireland in anticipation of the coming into effect of EC directives.

The Central Bank has had a relatively short period of relevant experience in carrying out its full range of responsibilities. The rapid evolution of central banking in Ireland over the past thirty years or so has been associated with the most serious monetary disturbances and the most significant structural changes in banking experienced in Ireland since the time of the Napoleonic wars and World War I. These disturbances and changes were the most significant experienced in peacetime conditions over the past 200 years and included major price increases, high volatile interest rates, fluctuating exchange rates, a rapid rate of structural change and increasing exposure to risk. Some of the monetary disturbances arose outside the economy and were to a large extent unavoidable. However, avoidable domestic developments made a major contribution to the monetary instability experienced between 1971 and 1987, in particular the emergence of large budget deficits which led to major external imbalances and very high levels of public debt

The current series of coins was introduced under the Decimal Currency Acts of 1969 and 1970. Three of the coins retain the 1928 designs on the obverse sides. Some of these coins may be replaced for a more convenient series in the future

expressed in foreign currencies, especially vis-à-vis non-residents.

Apart from these adverse experiences, it is noteworthy that the development of the Irish economy has advanced more since the 1950s than over the previous century and a half. However, it is not all that surprising that it was during adverse domestic monetary conditions, together with the experiences arising from ending the fixed link with sterling and those associated with the major structural changes in banks in recent decades, that led to central banking reaching maturity in the Republic. The experiences of recent decades have also prepared the way for full participation by the Central Bank in the evolving European central banking arrangements, which will gain momentum in the decades ahead.

NORTHERN IRELAND: BANKING AND THE AUTHORITIES

Broadly speaking, banking in Northern Ireland was not brought within the direct influence of the monetary authority (namely, the Bank of England) before the early 1970s, when similar liquidity requirements for banks were introduced in both Britain and Northern Ireland. Their application was less onerous in Northern Ireland. Again, in the early 1980s the revisions to the liquidity arrangements in Britain were not applied with full vigour in Northern Ireland, where the banks are being required to hold only half the level of liquidity (in the form of non-interest bearing balances at the Bank of England) compared with banks in Britain. Thus, since the early 1970s, a more direct interest has been shown by the Bank of England, although the Northern Ireland banks did not have to adhere to the quantitative limit on the growth in bank lending applied in Britain during the 1970s.

The main thrust of monetary and interest rate policy in Northern Ireland comes directly and continuously through external financial markets and through changes in the magnitude of the liquid assets of the Northern Ireland banks held outside Northern Ireland. What this means in effect is that the level of, and changes in, interest rates in Northern Ireland have been following without delay those in the sterling markets in London. It also means that the liquid assets of banks and other financial institutions in Northern Ireland have continued to consist primarily of sterling claims on the London financial markets rather than on local institutions, as one would expect with full monetary integration between Northern Ireland and its main trading partner, Britain.

Finally, it is appropriate to mention that, since 1979, the banks in Northern Ireland fall fully within the scope of the Bank of England's evolving supervisory arrangements; other major financial institutions or activities in Northern Ireland are supervised by appropriate British supervisory authorities or by reference to the supervisory standards applied in Britain. Thus, where relevant, the major legally underpinned changes in the supervision of financial activities that are being introduced in Britain in the 1980s are also being extended to Northern Ireland. Recent examples of this were the transfer, from 1 January 1987, of supervisory responsibility for building societies registered in Northern Ireland to the Building Societies Commission in London and the application of the provisions of the Financial Services Act 1986 to Northern Ireland institutions. Full financial integration with Britain over the years has resulted in a greater proportion of the financial services consumed in Northern Ireland being provided from outside its economy. This contrasts with the experiences of the Republic where, in recent decades, the domestic production of financial services, including those exported, has been playing a larger role in the economy.

The Central Bank of Ireland moved into its current premises on Dame Street in 1978

PART III

TOWARDS
THE TWENTY-FIRST
CENTURY

1990s AND BEYOND

While one cannot predict the future, present tendencies evolve into the future. The emphasis here is on the longer term perspective — on the general direction in which the banking and other financial institutions are currently moving rather than on the shorter term concerns that require immediate attention. Such concerns include making the most of the opportunities being offered by the emerging single market in Europe; establishing IFOX — the recently launched Irish Futures and Options Exchange; reforming the operation and supervision of the Stock Exchange in Ireland; developing the International Financial Services Centre; implementing the significant body of legislation, both domestic and EC, that is being finalised and enacted in advance of 1992; and strengthening the supervision of all credit institutions, securities and investment activities and the insurance industry. Financial institutions will continue to specialise in extending credit, managing savings, providing payments services, processing information, offering advice and acting as custodians of assets. But the manner in which these activities are performed will continue to change.

FUTURE PAYMENTS AND SAVINGS FACILITIES

Historical experience indicates that privately issued money eventually comes under the control of the authorities who become involved in producing it and determining the total amount that it is desirable to issue. This has happened in the case of coins and currency notes over the centuries. Even as far back as 1500, privately owned mints were prohibited from striking coins for the private sector. Similarly, during the past 150 years, most privately owned banks have had to relinquish the right to issue their own currency notes or only continue to do so provided the profits accrued to the state.

Provision of currency has come under the direct influence of the state. This ensures that the state has control over the production of and access to the resources and profits from issuing notes and coins, the promotion of confidence and uniformity in the composition of the currency, the fostering of efficient arrangements for effecting payments and the availability of an adequate supply of money to support non-inflationary economic growth. The same issues will be to the fore when the development of integrated, European-wide central banking arrangements gains further momentum.

A feature of the evolution of financial systems over the centuries is that innovations in financial products result in the more recently introduced payments and savings facilities growing more rapidly than the longer established facilities. Coins and currency notes have been declining over the decades as a proportion of the total means of payments because of the relatively rapid growth of current and deposit account money. In recent times, substitutes for credit balances on current and deposit accounts have been emerging rapidly and are likely to gain momentum in the decades ahead.

It may not be too far-fetched to suggest that in the early decades of the next century, money (in the form of credit balances with financial institutions) that is circulated by the widespread use of multipurpose, prepaid plastic cards may be regarded as the 'small change' of the economy. Furthermore, a new form of banking institution may emerge with the simultaneous extension of credit and provision of general-purpose prepaid plastic cards to those with a demand for this combination of facilities. Moreover, money in this form may be produced and issued by reference to public utility or public interest standards rather than by private institutions whose motivations are primarily technological and profit oriented. The desires and attitudes of the past, that brought about and retained the production and issue of notes and coins under the influence of the authorities over the centuries, will probably continue to prevail and determine how the 'small change' of the economy is produced and issued in the opening decades of the next century.

In the years ahead, central banks will probably acquire extended responsibilities on several fronts. They may be required to concentrate, to a greater extent than before, on the implications of innovations in the financial markets, to develop new techniques for managing the growth of the technologically based means of payments and to assess the impact of the innovations in payments methods on the level of spending. Central banks will also have to concern themselves with the reliability and integrity of the clearing and ultimate settlement arrangements associated with securities and other financial assets, and with the technologically based payments systems of the future. One can conceive of payments systems that lead to the synchronisation of the payments and receipts associated with the exchange of income and assets. Money could thus become redundant.

The realisation of this is a long way off because of the inherent vulnerability of settlement and payments systems. There will be an ongoing concern in society by those receiving payments that those initiating the payments will have the ready capacity to give instantaneous financial and legal effect to them. Consequently, the bulk of transactions, for a long time to come, will continue to be effected by conventional means of payment in which people have confidence that the payment converts into an asset whose acceptability is guaranteed throughout society.

The écu originated in France in about 1266, when Louis IX (Saint Louis) issued the 'écu d'or' which was used throughout Europe. The obverse of the coin (top) shows six fleurs de lys in an eight-lobed rosette. Only seven of these beautiful coins survive. Other écus were minted in France and other European countries up until the 18th century

In the meantime, reliable technological developments that reduce the costs, time required and inconvenience of effecting widely acceptable methods of settlement and payment, both domestically and internationally, are to be welcomed. However, the most efficient, computer-based private sector settlement and payment facilities will require the ultimate support of central banks well into the future if society is to continue to maximise the benefits to it of widely or generally acceptable monetary means of payments.

Such tendencies could result in the credit balances on current, deposit and analogous accounts that are actively used in effecting payments evolving towards a position in which they have the backing of the state. Similarly, the unutilised value of multipurpose, prepaid plastic cards may also evolve towards a position in which they have the support of the state. This would happen because of concern about the ultimate quality of the means of payment used in society which, in the past, led to state backing for coins, notes and, indeed, for the banks' deposits with the Central Bank. Such a development could have significant implications for the future structure of the banking institutions in the private sector, including associated card-issuing facilities. It could channel a significant part of their business closer to the non-bank financial institutions and into securities-related areas, with the central bank being less concerned about their commitments and ability to discharge their liabilities in respect of these activities.

Furthermore, fixed-valued claims (other than coins, notes and balances embodied in or associated with the technologically based payments arrangements) may become relatively less important. Savers may then be relying upon an extended range of variable-value savings facilities, offered by a wide variety of financial institutions, to maximise the benefits from diversifying their financial assets. At the same time, borrowers may be drawing on a greater variety of financing techniques and cultivating a wider range of sources of funds, with a view to minimising their funding costs. Indeed, banking as we know it today may not be easy to recognise in the opening decades of the next century.

CREDIT AND THE CREATION OF MONEY

A recurring international debate since the beginning of the last century, both in the professional literature and among policy-makers, is the issue of whether or not newly emerging financial arrangements and institutions have the capacity to create additional money by extending credit. Apart from the Central Bank, the banks are the only existing credit institutions that are officially recognised as having the capacity to create money. Total lending by banking institutions is regarded as adding to the stock of money in existence, even though part of bank lending only results in financial intermediation, that is, the reintroduction of money into circulation that had already been withdrawn through the accumulation by savers of credit balances with banks.

Another way of looking at this process is that matching increases in customers' borrowings from, and deposits with, passively oriented banks (that is, increases that are not associated with significant changes in borrowers' perceptions towards risk or in savers' preferences) may be regarded as neutral financial intermediation. But matching increases in bank lending and deposits that arise from deliberate policy initiatives by banks to increase the risk they undertake, and that lead to a greater willingness by bank customers to increase their borrowings and holdings of deposits, may be regarded as the genuine creation of money by way of lending, rather than neutral intermediation as described above. Changes in the state of confidence and attitudes towards bearing risk and credit-worthiness go a long way in helping to distinguish between what is financial intermediation and the creation of money through the extension of credit.

However, one does not know where to break into the circle. In practice, it is impossible to distinguish between the element of bank lending that is neutral in its impact on the amount of money in circulation and that part which leads to an increase in it. It is because the latter element is regarded, in the light of experience, as being significant in the case of banks that monetary policy concerns itself primarily with the growth in bank lending rather than with a wider range of lending or borrowing facilities.

With the evolution of the financial sector, an increasing variety of financial institutions may be coming to the fore. The new institutions may increase in size and extend credit with increasing confidence in their ability to finance simultaneously part of it by attracting savings, especially if they offer savings facilities that are also used more extensively in effecting payments. In this manner, they will probably develop the capacity to influence independently the level of national spending, especially at the time of a relatively rapid rate of growth in their lending.

From the point of view of the implementation of monetary policy, the more recently established or more rapidly growing institutions will be eventually considered as equivalent to the longer established banks. Past examples of this type of development in Ireland include the incorporation at the end of the 1960s of clearing bank lending that was matched by increases in their domestic deposit liabilities within the scope of credit policy guidelines; the placing, around the same time, of lending by the recently launched or established banks on a similar footing to that of the clearing banks for monetary policy purposes; and, in the last century, the placing of limitations in the 1840s on the issue of private bank notes unless backed by gold.

Looking to the future, building societies, the Agricultural Credit Corporation, the Industrial Credit Company, trustee savings banks and other non-bank deposit-taking institutions may evolve in such a manner. They will probably be considered as having the capacity to create additional money by extending credit, especially if regarded as a single group of institutions, with the result that it may be appropriate to bring them within the direct scope of monetary policy. This may be because of their enhanced ability to influence the process of creating money, their contribution to the provision of facilities for effecting payments and their potential capacity to rely excessively from time to time on the short-term lending facility of the Central Bank.

It is probable that a debate about the respective roles and influences of banks and other credit institutions in the economy will be reopened during the 1990s. This will arise as the frontiers of what constitutes banking activity and the capacity to create money are pushed outwards, as has occurred on a number of occasions over the past two hundred years.

SECURITIES ACTIVITIES: MONETARY IMPLICATIONS

Apart from the increasing variety of financial institutions, there is an additional development occurring — wealth, in the form of money and financial assets, is accumulating. The management of financial assets and securities is growing in importance and different types are becoming more marketable with the evolution of the markets. The markets for diversified financial assets, issued by a wider variety of borrowers, will probably be a more important feature of the financial sector by the beginning of the next century. The purchase and sale of existing assets (that is, asset switching) will probably continue to be regarded as neutral in its effects on the supply of money. But the liquidity (or ability to be readily converted into cash) of such securities may be enhanced with more competitive conditions for making markets, trading and determining the prices of securities. However, in the 1990s, the emphasis will probably be on security selection and international diversification of portfolios over the medium term rather than on short-term trading that is motivated by the emergence of small temporary differences in prices of securities, as was the experience when prices of most securities were increasing simultaneously in the 1980s.

LEVERAGE
The relationship between the magnitude of shareholders' or owners' funds in a company and the amount borrowed by the company. Also referred to as the 'gearing ratio'. Generally, the greater the amount of borrowing or liabilities relative to a given amount of capital or financial commitments by the owner or investor, the higher the leverage or gearing, and the greater the degree of risk associated with increases in interest rates and downturns in business.

A debate could also emerge, alongside the bank *versus* other credit institutions debate, about the monetary implications of the growth of the stock of marketable securities that facilitates the bypassing of the banks and other credit institutions in the channelling of funds from savers to borrowers. A relatively rapid increase over a short period of time in the diversified stock of marketable domestic securities in existence may be considered, up to a point, as having some money-creation characteristics.

This might well be the situation if securities were being issued and widely distributed with enthusiasm, supported by market-making arrangements and held by investors with a high degree of confidence that ultimate settlement would occur within a few days. It would not come as a complete surprise if such developments came to be regarded, in the opening decades of the next century, as capable of making a small independent contribution to increasing the stream of spending in the economy. The definition and identification of what is mainly credit creation, intermediation, banking and non-banking financial activities will continue to be elusive in the decades ahead, especially with a growing proportion of the domestic demand for these services being accommodated from abroad.

An increase in exposure to risk, by way of, for example, large exposures, extended leverages, multiple ranges of activities and wider gaps or longer distances between primary savers and ultimate borrowers, will accompany the technology developments, financial innovations, complicated institutional growth and the more competitive conditions suggested here. Completion should lead to an all-round narrowing of margins throughout the financial sector and to greater concentration within it. Thus, ongoing changes in the supervision of the financial sector, as has been occurring, will continue to be necessary as the financial sector evolves along the lines discussed.

SUPERVISORY REQUIREMENTS: SPECIALISATION AND COOPERATION

The main objective of supervision is to avoid systemic instability at the same time as the benefits of innovation and the evolution of the financial sector are realised in an internationally competitive environment. While significant changes will occur in the supervisory arrangements against the background of EC directives to be introduced in the early 1990s, the emphasis here is on the need for continuity in the evolution of supervision to keep pace with the ongoing changes that will occur in the financial sector. The indications are that there will continue to be three main areas within the financial sector which will require specific supervisory skills and capacity. In reality, these requirements will be much more complicated with the emergence of cross-frontier financial supermarkets that, in turn, may be only one element of multipurpose, worldwide holding companies.

Firstly, the banks and other credit institutions that accept deposits, manage the payments systems, extend credit and create money should continue to be supervised by the Central Bank because of the nature of their activities. Apart from the extension of the Central Bank's supervision to all credit institutions, greater emphasis will need to be given in the years ahead to the supervision of the provision of plastic-card money. Supervision of credit institutions will also need to keep evolving as these institutions develop further towards becoming financial supermarkets themselves and part of wider financial groupings.

This will entail the extension of supervision to the growing range of activities of the credit institution itself and its subsidiaries, to the activities of the holding company of which the credit institution itself is a subsidiary and to sister companies that are also subsidiaries of the same holding company as the credit institution itself. Directors and management, who are ultimately responsible for the safety and soundness of a bank or credit institution, will have greater burdens placed on them to ensure that the exposure of the institution to risk is fully taken into account and controlled. These responsibilities will become more difficult to discharge with the growing range of diverse activities undertaken, the increasing scope for conflicts of interest and the emergence of more complicated corporate structures.

CONFLICTS OF INTEREST
A situation can arise in which two or more interests are legitimately present and compete with each other. Steps are taken within companies to minimise such conflicts, by limiting the range of functions undertaken and by placing legal and behavioural barriers to the transfer of information from those involved in a particular function to those engaged in other functions within the company. Greater competition would help to reduce conflicts of interest, especially if customer loyalty were weakened.

Despite a growing proportion of the assets of credit institutions becoming more marketable and less of their liabilities being repayable on demand at predetermined fixed values, it would seem appropriate also that credit institutions continue to have the support of the temporary lender-of-last-resort facility. Such a facility should continue to be regarded as a safety valve to avoid the excessively costly adjustment of otherwise solvent credit institutions. Given the appropriateness of a central bank avoiding the provision of temporary public support to a wide range of non-credit financial institutions, securities firms and other non-bank financial institutions, the lender-of-last-resort facility should be confined to the credit institutions with an inherently large non-marketable portfolio and with an indisputable capacity to create money by granting credit.

The second area within the financial sector that will continue to require specific supervisory arrangements is insurance. It may be necessary to keep this area separate as significant risks, which are not readily diversifiable, will continue to be centred in this part of the financial sector. While the savings facilities provided by banks and life assurance companies will probably lead to a blurring of the distinction between these institutions, the management of the liquidity needs of assurance companies is less demanding than in the case of banks, owing to the relatively longer term contractual nature of savings in the form of life assurance. However, it is likely that pure or general insurance business and banking will continue to be so different as to require separate arrangements.

The market value of a bank's assets (much of which consists of non-transferable loans) is not as predictable as those of a general insurance company (which include a high proportion of transferable assets). In valuing their assets, banks must rely mainly on their own ability to predict and measure the capacity of their customers to repay, whereas insurance companies can draw to a greater extent on the outside markets as an aid in valuing their assets. On the other hand, the withdrawals of cash or calls upon the liabilities of a bank are more predictable than those on a general insurance company. This would be the case particularly if the latter concentrated on the larger, once-off type of risks rather than on the more generalised smaller risks that are widespread throughout society and amenable to reasonably frequent review. Insurance companies that underwrite large risk business can be confronted with major claims that are very difficult to predict, both in respect of magnitude and timing. Such claims could fully absorb not only the cash flow from ongoing business, but also lead to the sale of substantial assets, thereby weakening the backing for the future commitments to policy-holders, which it would be difficult to redress.

The predictability of a bank's liabilities is related more closely to savings-motivated behaviour than are the claims on a general insurance company. In the case of general insurance companies, the exercise of certain types of claims on them can be spread unevenly and unpredictably over a number of years because of the very nature of certain types of insurance risks that are not easy to recognise in advance and which cannot be diversified or spread to any substantial extent. This is because the exercise of claims on insurance companies depends more on the random occurrence of events of nature, statutory requirements and interpretations thereof and the laws of probability rather than on the more predictable human actions that are primarily profit-oriented or economically motivated.

The safety valves appropriate to the insurance industry put much greater reliance than banks on

REINSURANCE
When a risk is considered by an insurance or assurance company to be relatively great, the company will lay off what it regards as the excess risk with a reinsurance company (or several companies) in order to diversify the risk.

SPOT OR CASH TRANSACTIONS
A purchase or sale of an asset for immediate delivery.

FORWARDS OR FUTURES
A purchase of an asset at a future date at a price that is fixed today is known as a forward or future transaction or contract. The term 'future' is usually reserved for standarised contracts that can be traded on an organised exchange or market; the term 'forward' refers to specially tailored contracts, arranged on a one-to-one basis, that are not tradeable on an organised exchange.

OPTIONS
Contracts which give the purchaser the right, but not the obligation, to either buy or sell an asset at a fixed price at a future date. The seller or writer of the option must respond if the purchaser exercises or utilises the option acquired. Options are a form of insurance for which the purchaser pays a premium to the seller.

prior assessment of the nature of the risks involved, appropriate pricing of the cover to be provided, scope for reviews and the spreading of risk by way of enforceable reinsurance. Banks rely to a much greater extent on prior understandings and capacity to borrow temporarily or dispose of liquid assets. These differences between banking and general insurance suggest that in order to maximise confidence in the financial system, it would seem appropriate to continue to support specialisation in the supervision of the fundamentally different types of financial institutions.

The third main area of the financial sector that will continue to require specific supervision is the capital markets, securities firms, portfolio management and other security and investment-related services. The distinguishing feature of this area is that the institutional arrangements are designed to allow liabilities to vary automatically in line with changes in the market value of assets, which can be volatile and unpredictable. While holders of securities cannot be protected from the effects of default by the issuers or ultimate borrowers behind such securities, supervision in this area should be concerned with the widespread availability of relevant information to facilitate continuous assessment of the prospects for the issuers of the securities.

Apart from the question of the exposure of the riskiness of the issuers of securities, supervision should also be concerned with the manner in which the spot or cash, futures and options markets for purchasing and selling existing securities, and claims thereon, continue to be organised, guaranteed and managed, so as to preserve the integrity of the exchanges and markets themselves. The continuous availability of information about the volumes and prices of securities traded, the distribution of exposures between member-firms and, in turn, between their customers, the timing of margin collections and the clearing and settlement of transactions or trades — all these factors should continue to be of ongoing concern to supervisors.

Furthermore, supervision of the securities industry should be concerned with the following in the case of firms that provide facilities for issuing, making markets, trading and managing portfolios of securities:

- ongoing capital requirements
- professional fitness
- liquidity and risk management ability
- client protection and compensation arrangements
- conduct of business rules, i.e. the standards to be applied in conducting business on behalf of customers, especially non-corporate customers
- the degree to which commissions and fees are competitively determined.

Consideration also needs to be given to the question of updating standards and requirements in respect of the growing range of investment and financial advisory services.

In the case of the evolving securities markets and related financial institutions, the appropriate safety valves to continue developing should include the extension and refinement of:

MARKING TO MARKET
The updating of the value of a marketable asset, or of a commitment or liability, by reference to recent market prices for the asset. Losses and gains are immediately highlighted.

- the prudent practices of marking-to-market, i.e. updating values by reference to the most up-to-date prices quoted
- the calling of margins or deposits without delay as prices change adversely in order to underwrite ability to perform
- the acceptance of the need for the ongoing commitment of the market-makers in adverse circumstances to continue buying and selling securities despite unfavourable movements in their prices
- the need to minimise the time lag between the date of the original purchase or sale of securities and the date of final settlement for them

SETTLEMENT RISK
The risk that operational difficulties may cause a delay in receiving delivery of funds or securities, and lead to a loss of income during the delay.

- the control and monitoring of risk exposures associated with the settlement of securities and other financial asset transactions
- the prompt provision of correct and timely information about volumes and prices of securities traded

- the capacity to halt trading without delay to assess the implications of recent large changes in prices
- the control of large exposures of single firms and, in turn, to single customers
- the promotion of closer cooperation between the organisations supporting and representing the different markets, exchanges and financial institutions.

The securities and investment-related activities are so diverse that they may not lend themselves to such streamlined supervisory arrangements as would be the case with banking and insurance. Indeed, as the banking industry has a special interest in securities-related activities, which will probably become much more important in the years ahead as bank assets themselves become more marketable, banking supervisors should be drawn further into the supervision of securities-related activities. The market-making activities of banks in the cash markets for securities, as well as their involvement with both futures and options activities, are important areas into which banking supervision should penetrate in evaluating the banks evolving overall risk-management policies and procedures. Close cooperation between these three main areas of supervisory responsibilities will be required in the decades ahead, but especially in relation to the supervision of credit institutions, capital markets and securities-related activities.

The theoretical literature needs to be reworked if it is to be a more useful guide to policy-makers concerned with the evolution of the financial sector. The theoretical expositions accounting for the existence and contribution of banking institutions, non-bank credit institutions, assurance and insurance underwriting and the securities industry should undergo fundamental changes in presentation during the decade ahead to give an integrated picture of the role of the different activities within the financial sector. It would also be helpful if this were accompanied by a reworking and development of the analytical foundations for the control and supervision, in the public interest, of the different types of financial activities (banking, non-bank credit institutions, securities and insurance) from both the monetary-policy and prudential-supervision perspectives.

Furthermore, it would be useful to evaluate the contribution of the evolving financial institutions and markets to investment and the accumulation of capital in the economy. In particular, with an increasing proportion of accumulating savings being managed by institutions rather than by the savers themselves, it would be appropriate to analyse the effects of this development on the allocation and use of savings.

Finally, the effectiveness of monetary policy in the less clearly defined future financial environment, as well as the scope and efficiency of the means or techniques used to implement it, must continue to be evaluated against the ultimate objectives of monetary policy. The avoidance of slippage in monetary control will be a major concern of central banks in Europe during the 1990s. These are challenging areas for future theoretical and, indeed, applied research, and for the formulation and implementation of policy.

INTEGRATING WITHIN EUROPE

The prospective developments outlined here will occur at the same time as financial and monetary integration is accelerating in Europe. The question is, to what extent the prospective developments in the Irish financial sector will be affected by the creation of a single financial market throughout Europe and the pursuit of the longer term goal of monetary union in Europe? As a matter of interest, initiatives towards monetary and financial union were also a significant feature of Europe in the second half of the nineteenth century. They were associated with the unification of Germany and Italy and the emergence of a central bank in those

Today, the ECU (or European Currency Unit) is a unit of account, used in EC transactions. The coin above was issued in 1987 in Belgium as a collector's item to commemorate the 30th anniversary of the Treaty of Rome

A cheque expressed in ECUs, the EC unit of account, not a medium of exchange

countries and also with three wider regional experiences or groupings — a Latin monetary union (between France, Belgium, Switzerland, Italy, Greece and a number of other countries), a Scandinavian monetary union (between Denmark, Norway and Sweden) and a German monetary union (embracing Germany and Austria). Adherence to the objectives and rules of the international gold standard in those days may have contributed to the establishment of monetary union independently of fiscal and economic integration in these regions.

In making further progress towards monetary union in the years ahead, European central banks will become more concerned with this objective and how it can be made a reality. They will be concentrating on the necessary conditions, operational arrangements and means available for successfully defending prevailing exchange rates and minimising inflation. This will call for greater coordination of interventions in the markets, to increase or reduce the supplies of individual European currencies in the context of agreed objectives between member-countries for the growth in Community-wide holdings of money and bank lending.

Such interventions will need to be consistent with minimising, or indeed avoiding, exchange rate adjustment between European currencies and maximising the non-inflationary growth of the base of the European banking system. It is in these circumstances that the main benefits of a single European currency — lower foreign exchange transactions costs, more confidence in the stability of prices and somewhat lower interest rates at home and throughout Europe — will begin to accrue to the Irish economy. However, in order to maximise these gains, economic and monetary union must be viewed as a single process, as agreed by the Delors Committee in its *Report on Economic and Monetary Union in the European Community,* published in 1989.

The process of European financial integration will gain significant momentum in the 1990s with the

implemention of the formidable legislative
programme to facilitate the completion of the single
financial market throughout Europe. Firms in the
Irish financial sector will find new opportunities to
become more externally oriented, to forge
appropriate cooperative relationships with financial
institutions abroad and to compete for an increasing
share of appropriate segments or areas of the more
integrated European financial market. The successful
establishment over time of a worthwhile presence
in specific areas of the European market will require
careful prior evaluation and, subsequently, a
continuous commitment on the part of
management. At the same time, the traditional home
and export markets will need to be defended as new
profitable markets abroad are penetrated.

Domestic and external growth objectives can be
pursued simultaneously by earning and raising
adequate capital to support the increased level and
range of activities. This needs to be accompanied
by investment in appropriate technologies and in
management and other manpower skills, and by the
narrowing of margins, especially between interest
received and paid, through greater efficiency in the
use of human resources and more effective control
of other non-interest costs. Over time, it is the low-
cost producers of high-quality products and services
with a coherent strategic commitment that will
continue to succeed in the struggle for increased
market share in appropriate segments of the
growing European-wide industry. Entry will
become freer, exit more frequent, output prices
lower and customers more demanding as the
national financial markets in Europe become more
integrated over the decade ahead.

Taxation policy, which takes account of the net
effect of all tax measures and is even-handed in its
approach to all domestic financial institutions,
would also contribute to the efficiency and growth
of the financial sector by ensuring that financial
activity bears a similar level of taxation in Ireland
as in the other member-states. Full financial
integration, without distortion of the location of

financial services activity, cannot take place without fiscal harmonisation in respect of savings and investment activities, of the profits of the financial institutions themselves and of the supporting disclosure requirements to the revenue authorities throughout Europe.

These developments will be accompanied by the evolution of a European-wide system of mutually recognised supervisory arrangements. This is already well advanced in the case of credit institutions and insurance companies; rapid progress is also being made in relation to a wide range of securities activities. It is envisaged that European-wide supervisory standards and arrangements will help to create and maintain similar conditions throughout Europe, thereby promoting greater competition between financial institutions and providing additional scope for locating the production of financial services where costs are relatively low and qualities are high. The supervision of financial conglomerates, whose activities embrace a wide range of diverse financial institutions in a number of European countries, will be a major challenge to the supervisory bodies of Europe.

It seems reasonable to conclude that what will be happening in Europe will serve primarily to accelerate some of the developments that would otherwise be occurring in the Irish financial sector. But the changes in Ireland will be taking place in an atmosphere of a deeper appreciation of the need to minimise the centralising forces at work on the road to economic and monetary union in Europe. These have been portrayed by the evolution over the past fifty years of the financial sector in Northern Ireland compared with that of the Republic.

If there is to be successful adaptation in a more competitive climate to the significant structural changes that will occur in the financial sector in the decades ahead, it will be necessary to address the issues outlined here about the future course of the financial sector. It will be important to ensure that the benefits to society of the prospective changes in the financial sector are realised without exposing the financial institutions to inappropriate risks and society to monetary instability. The formulation and implementation of monetary policy and prudential supervision of the financial sector will continue to be a major and rewarding challenge to those involved in central banking, both at the national and European levels.

CHRONOLOGY

990s	Coins introduced into circulation in Viking Dublin.
1200s	Normans issue coins with increasing frequency.
1200 to 1450	Irish and English coins, though different in design, exchanged at par.
1460	Coinage devalued and Irish currency recognised independently for first time.
1534-36	Currency devalued and Harp coinage introduced into circulation by Henry VIII.
1601	Copper coinage introduced by Elizabeth I. Sharp, temporary depreciation of exchange rate between 1601 and 1603.
1650s	Irish and English currencies temporarily united at par.
1680s to 1720s	Currency notes introduced gradually in form of receipts issued by goldsmiths and merchants.
1689	Reform of Irish currency, leading to a fixed rate of exchange (13 Irish to 12 English) which prevailed without interruption for over 100 years.
1720s	Little political support for innovations in coinage and banking, including the establishment of a national or central bank, in the aftermath of the South Sea Bubble crisis.
1756	Legislation passed to exclude merchants engaged in foreign trade from acting as bankers.
1783	Bank of Ireland (today, a clearing bank) established in Dublin by Irish Parliament. It was the only corporate body in Ireland with the right to issue currency notes for the next 40 years or so.
1797	Irish currency floated against gold, sterling and other currencies. Sharp fluctuations in exchange rate experienced over next 24 years.
1797-1803	Substantial increases in Exchequer borrowing, bank lending and currency notes outstanding, together with a 10% depreciation in the exchange rate.
1815	The first savings bank established in Stillorgan, Co. Dublin. The existing trustee savings banks were established before 1820.
1817	Amalgamation of Irish and British Exchequers and Public Debts.
1821	Fixed exchange rate reintroduced with re-establishment of convertibility of Irish bank notes into gold at same rate as in 1797. Bank of Ireland's sole right to issue notes throughout the country confined to a radius of 65 miles from Dublin.
1824	Northern Banking Company founded in Belfast.

1825   Hibernian Bank founded in Dublin. Provincial Bank of Ireland founded, with head office in London. Bank note exchange established between banks.

1826   Amalgamation of Irish and English currencies at parity (an arrangement that continues to exist between Northern Ireland and Britain). British notes and coins, including sovereigns, circulated freely throughout Ireland, alongside the note issue of the Irish clearing banks, until 1928.

1827   Belfast Banking Company established in Belfast.

1834   National Bank of Ireland founded, with head office in London.

1836   Royal Bank of Ireland founded in Dublin. Ulster Bank founded in Belfast.

1845   The Bankers' (Ireland) Act 1845 stipulated that any further increase in a bank's currency notes must be fully backed by gold and silver rather than with loans, securities and balances with banks. Act also provided that all note-issuing banks could issue their notes within the Dublin region, in competition with the Bank of Ireland. Clearing arrangements for cheques introduced by banks.

1848   Legislation passed requiring appointment of auditors to savings banks.

1861   Post Office Savings Bank established by authorities.

1885   Munster and Leinster Bank founded in Cork following failure of Munster Bank.

1914   Irish bank notes temporarily extended legal tender status on 5 August. Prices increase sharply over the period 1914 to 1919.

1917   Belfast Banking Company acquired by London City and Midland Bank on 1 July; a few months later, Ulster Bank acquired by the London County and Westminster Bank.

1920   Legal tender status withdrawn from Irish bank notes with effect from 1 January.

1926   Coinage Act 1926 becomes law on 13 April. Act repealed in 1951.

1927   Currency Act 1927 becomes law on 20 August. Act repealed in 1989. Currency Commission (forerunner of Central Bank) established on 21 September.

1928   Bankers' (Northern Ireland) Act 1928 becomes law on 2 July. Irish legal tender notes issued to public on 10 September. Irish coins introduced into circulation on 12 December. Repatriation of British currency from Republic commences.

1929   Issue of bank notes by clearing banks in Republic terminated with effect from 6 May. However, each clearing bank was allowed to issue what were described as Consolidated Bank Notes ('ploughman' notes) up to a specified limit; these notes did not enjoy legal tender status.

1943   Central Bank of Ireland established on 1 February, when main provisions of Central Bank Act 1942 came into effect.

1953   Issue of Consolidated Bank Notes terminated with effect from 31 December.

1956   Exchequer Bills rediscounted by Central Bank for first time in January.

1958   Hibernian Bank acquired by Bank of Ireland in December.

1965   Central Bank introduces credit guidelines for clearing banks on 13 May. Northern Bank acquired by Midland Bank with effect from 27 May.

1966   Business of National Bank Ltd in Republic and Northern Ireland acquired by Bank of Ireland on 9 March. Allied Irish Bank incorporated on 21 September, following a merger agreement between boards of Munster and Leinster Bank, Provincial Bank of Ireland and Royal Bank of Ireland.

1969   Most of the external assets of clearing banks transferred to Central Bank during August.

1970   Central Bank extends credit guidelines to non-clearing banks on 17 April. Clearing banks closed to public from 30 April to 17 November because of a labour dispute between them and the Irish Bank Officials' Association. Northern Bank absorbs Belfast Banking Company on 1 July.

1971   Decimal currency system comes into effect on 15 February. Central Bank Act 1971 effective from 1 September which, *inter alia,* provided for the licensing and supervision of banks.

1972   Exchequer Account transferred from Bank of Ireland to Central Bank on 1 January. Central Bank announces on 2 June that official liquidity ratios for banks are to be introduced.

1978   Participation in the European Monetary System (EMS) announced on 15 December. Exchange controls extended to Northern Ireland, Britain, Channel Islands and Isle of Man with effect from 18 December.

1979   EMS comes into operation on 13 March. Maintenance of the one-for-one parity between Irish pound and sterling discontinued on 30 March.

1985   Insurance Corporation of Ireland plc placed under Administration, following announcement on 15 March, and ceases to be a wholly owned subsidiary of Allied Irish Bank. Each clearing bank free from end of May to determine independently its structure of interest rates.

1986   Downward adjustment of 8% in bilateral central rate of Irish pound against other EMS currencies announced on 2 August. Trustee Savings Bank of Northern Ireland privatised in September.

1988   All exchange control restrictions on the purchase of medium and long-term foreign securities by Irish residents removed with effect from end of 1988.

1989   Central Bank becomes responsible for supervision of building societies, futures and options exchange, money brokers and certain financial institutions in the International Financial Services Centre, with the coming into effect of the Central Bank Act 1989 on 12 July and the Building Societies Act 1989 on 1 September.

BIBLIOGRAPHY

Aaronovitch, Sam and Samson, Peter. *The Insurance Industry in the Countries of the EEC.* Luxembourg: Office for Official Publications of the European Communities, 1985.

Barrow, G.L. *The Emergence of the Irish Banking System: 1820-1845.* Dublin: Gill and Macmillan, 1975.

Barrow, G.L. 'The Irish Banking System in 1845'. *Central Bank of Ireland, Quarterly Bulletin* No. 2, 1975, pp. 92-111.

Barrow, G.L. 'The Use of Money in Mid-Nineteenth Century Ireland'. *Studies,* Spring 1970, pp. 81-8.

Barry, Kevin. 'The Central Bank's Management of the Aggregrate Liquidity of Licensed Banks'. *Central Bank of Ireland, Annual Report,* 1983, pp. 104-15.

Bourke, Philip and Kinsella, R.P. *The Financial Services Revolution: An Irish Perspective.* Dublin: Gill and Macmillan, 1988.

Breen, Bernard J. 'Some Thoughts on Financial Markets and Interest Rates'. *Central Bank of Ireland, Quarterly Bulletin* No. 2, 1980, pp. 48-52.

Brennan, Joseph. 'Monetary Functions of Commercial Banks'. *Journal of The Statistical and Social Inquiry Society of Ireland,* Vol. XVII, 1942-43, pp. 62-84.

Brennan, Joseph. 'The Currency System of the Irish Free State'. *Journal of The Statistical and Social Inquiry Society of Ireland,* Vol. XV, 1930-31, pp. 23-32.

Browne, F.X. 'A Monthly Money Market Model for Ireland in the EMS'. *Central Bank of Ireland, Annual Report,* 1986, pp. 76-117.

Browne, F.X. and O'Connell, T. 'A Quantitative Analysis of the Degree of Integration between Irish and UK Financial Markets'. *The Economic and Social Review,* Vol. 9, No. 4, July 1978, pp. 283-300.

Casey, Michael. 'Monetary Modelling in Ireland'. *Central Bank of Ireland, Annual Report,* 1985, pp. 82-109.

Central Bank of Ireland. 'Licensing and Supervision Requirements and Standards for Banks'. *Central Bank of Ireland, Quarterly Bulletin* No. 3, 1987, pp. 60-70.

Challis, C.E. 'The Tudor Coinage for Ireland'. *British Numismatic Journal,* Vol. XL, 1971.

Cleeve, Brian (Ed.). *W.B. Yeats and the Designing of Ireland's Coinage.* Dublin: Dolmen Press, 1972.

Cork Historical and Archaeological Society. 'The Cork Savings Bank 1817-1917'. *Journal of the Cork Historical and Archaeological Society,* Oct-Dec. 1918.

Cullen, L.M. *An Economic History of Ireland since 1660*. London: B.T. Batsford, 1987 (2nd edition).

Cullen, L.M. 'The Pound from Harp to Snake'. *The Irish Times*, 4 August 1986.

Cullen, L.M. 'Landlords, Bankers and Merchants: The Early Irish Banking World, 1700-1820'. In *Economists and the Irish Economy from the Eighteenth Century to the Present Day*, Antoin E. Murphy (Ed.). Dublin: Irish Academic Press, 1984.

Davy Kelleher McCarthy. *The Control of Banking in the Republic of Ireland*. Dublin: Davy Kelleher McCarthy, 1984.

Deale, A. *The Pioneer Savings Banks of the 1800s*. Dublin: Dublin Savings Bank, 1946.

De Cecco, Marcello and Giovannini, Alberto. *A European Central Bank? Perspectives on Monetary Unification after ten years of the EMS*. Cambridge: Cambridge University Press, 1989.

Dowling, Brendan R. 'The Development of the Financial Sector in Ireland, 1949-1972'. *Journal of The Statistical and Social Inquiry Society of Ireland*, Vol. XXIII, Part I, 1973-74, pp. 57-107.

Doyle, Maurice F. 'Developments in the Financial Sector: Some Supervisory Implications'. *Central Bank of Ireland, Quarterly Bulletin* No. 2, 1988, pp. 48-62.

Eason, C. 'The Trustee Savings Banks of Great Britain and Ireland'. *Journal of The Statistical and Social Inquiry Society of Ireland*, Vol. XIV, 1929-30, pp. 1-24.

European Communities. Committee for the Study of Economic and Monetary Union, 1989. *Report on Economic and Monetary Union in the European Community*. Luxembourg: Office for Official Publications of the European Communities, 1989.

Fanning, Ronan. *The Irish Department of Finance 1922-58*. Dublin: Institute of Public Administration, 1978.

Fetter, Frank W. *Development of British Monetary Orthodoxy 1797-1875*. Cambridge, MA: Harvard University Press, 1965.

Fetter, Frank W. *The Irish Pound 1797-1826*. London: Allen and Unwin, 1955.

Foster, R.F. *Modern Ireland 1600-1972*. London: Allen Lane/Penguin Press, 1988.

Giavazzi, Francesco and Giovannini, Alberto. *Limiting Exchange Rate Flexibility: The European Monetary System*. Cambridge, MA: The MIT Press, 1989.

Gibson, Norman J. *The Financial System in Northern Ireland*. Belfast: Northern Ireland Economic Council, 1982, Report No. 29.

Gibson, Norman J. 'The Irish and British Pounds: Old and New Relationships'. *The Three Banks Review*, March 1980, pp. 49-63.

Gibson, Norman J. 'An Amended Irish Monetary System'. *Journal of The Statistical and Social Inquiry Society of Ireland*, Vol. XIX, Part 5, 1956-57, pp. 137-64.

Goodhart, Charles. *Money Information and Uncertainty*. London: Macmillian Education Ltd, 1989 (2nd edition).

Goodhart, Charles. *The Evolution of Central Banks*. Cambridge, MA: MIT Press, 1988 (2nd edition).

Hall, F.G. *The Bank of Ireland 1783-1946*. Dublin: Hodges Figgis, 1949.

Haughton, Jonathan. 'The Historical Background'. In *The Economy of Ireland*, John W. O'Hagan (Ed.). Dublin: Irish Management Institute, 1987 (5th edition), pp. 1-51.

Hill, Edwin Darley. *The Northern Banking Company Limited: Centenary Volume, 1824-1924*. Belfast: McCaw, Stevenson & Orr, 1925.

Hoare, T.F. 'Nature and Functions of an Irish Money Market. *Journal of The Statistical and Social Inquiry Society of Ireland*, Vol. XXII, Part 2, 1969-70, pp. 1-27.

Horne, Oliver H. *A History of Savings Banks*. London: Oxford University Press, 1947.

Institute of Bankers in Ireland. *Global Financial Services and their Role in Banking in the 1990s*. Papers presented to the 42nd International Banking Summer School, Ireland, July-August 1989. Dublin: Institute of Bankers in Ireland, 1989.

Kennedy, Kieran A., Giblin, Thomas and McHugh, Deirdre. *The Economic Development of Ireland in the Twentieth Century*. London & New York: Routledge and Kegan Paul, 1988.

Knox, William J. *Decades of the Ulster Bank 1836-1964*. Belfast: Bell, Logan and Carswell, 1965.

Lee, Joseph. 'The Dual Economy in Ireland 1800-1850'. *Historical Studies*, Vol. VIII, 1971.

Lee, Joseph. 'Capital in the Irish Economy'. In *The Formation of the Irish Economy*, L.M. Cullen (Ed.). Cork: Mercier Press, 1969.

Lyons, F.S.L. (Ed.). *Bicentenary Essays, Bank of Ireland 1783-1983*. Dublin: Gill and Macmillan, 1983.

McCormack, Dara. 'Policy-making in a Small Open Economy: Some Aspects of Irish Experience'. *Central Bank of Ireland, Quarterly Bulletin* No. 4, 1979, pp. 92-113.

McDowell, Moore J. 'The Devaluation of 1460 and the Origins of the Irish Pound'. *Irish Historical Studies*, Vol. XXV, No. 97, May 1986.

McElligott, J.J. 'President's Inaugural Address to the Institute of Bankers in Ireland'. *Journal of the Institute of Bankers in Ireland*, April 1956.

McGowan, Padraig. 'Monetary Implications of European Integration'. *The Irish Banking Review,* Winter 1986, pp. 35-46.

Meenan, James. *The Irish Economy since 1922.* Liverpool: Liverpool University Press, 1970.

Milne, Kenneth. *A History of the Royal Bank of Ireland Limited.* Dublin: Allen Figgis, 1964.

Mitchenson, Rosalind and Roebuck, Peter (Eds.). *Economy and Society in Scotland and Ireland 1500-1939.* Edinburgh: John McDonald Publishers, 1988.

Moynihan, Maurice. *Currency and Central Banking in Ireland 1922-1960.* Dublin: Gill and Macmillan/Central Bank of Ireland, 1975.

Munn, C.W. 'The Emergence of Central Banking in Ireland: The Bank of Ireland 1814-1850'. *Irish Economic and Social History,* Vol. X, 1983.

Murray, C.H. 'The European Monetary System: Implications for Ireland'. *Central Bank of Ireland, Annual Report,* 1979, pp. 96-108.

O'Brien, George. 'The Last Years of the Irish Currency'. *Economic History Supplement to Economic Journal,* May 1927.

Ó Cofaigh, Tomás F. 'Irish Banking: A Forward View'. *Central Bank of Ireland, Quarterly Bulletin* No. 2, 1986, pp. 63-9.

O'Connell, Thomas. 'The Central Bank: Monetary Policy and Financial Regulation'. *Central Bank of Ireland, Quarterly Bulletin* No. 2, 1988, pp. 72-86.

Ó Gráda, Cormac. *The Paper Pounds of 1797-1821: A Co-Integration Analysis.* Dublin: Centre for Economic Research, University College Dublin, Working Paper No. 11, 1989.

Ó Gráda, Cormac. *Ireland before and after the Famine: Explorations in Economic History 1800-1925.* Manchester: Manchester University Press, 1988.

O'Grady Walshe, Timothy. 'President's Inaugural Address to the Institute of Bankers in Ireland'. *Journal of the Institute of Bankers in Ireland,* Vol. 1, No. 1, Spring 1989.

O'Kelly, Eoin. *The Old Private Banks and Bankers of Munster.* Cork: Cork University Press, 1959.

Ollerenshaw, Philip. *Banking in Nineteenth-Century Ireland: The Belfast Banks 1825-1914.* Manchester: Manchester University Press, 1988.

Ollerenshaw, Philip. 'Industy 1820-1914'. In *An Economic History of Ulster 1820-1939,* Liam Kennedy and Philip Ollerenshaw (Eds.). Manchester: Manchester University Press, 1985, pp. 96-102.

O'Shea, James. 'Thurles Savings Bank 1829-1871'. In *Thurles: The Cathedral Town,* William Corbett and William Nolan (Eds.). Dublin: Geography Publications, 1989.

Oslizlok, J.S. 'Survey of Sources of Monetary Supplies in Ireland'.

Journal of The Statistical and Social Inquiry Society of Ireland, Vol. XXI, Part 1, 1962-63, pp. 109-34.

Pratschke, John L. 'The Establishing of the Irish Pound: A Backward Glance'. *Economic and Social Review,* Vol. 1, No. 1, October 1969, pp. 51-75.

Ryan, W.J.L. *Report of the Money Market Committee under the Chairmanship of W.J.L. Ryan.* Dublin: Central Bank of Ireland, 1969.

Share, Bernard (Ed.). *Root and Branch: Allied Irish Banks Yesterday, Today and Tomorrow.* Dublin: AIB, 1979.

Simpson, Noel. *The Belfast Bank 1827-1970.* Belfast: Blackstaff Press, 1975.

Smiddy, T.A. 'Some Reflections on Commercial Banks, with special reference to the Balance Sheets of Banks operating in Saorstát Éireann'. *Journal of The Statistical and Social Inquiry Society of Ireland,* Vol. XV, 1935-36, pp. 53-68a.

Thomas, W.A. *The Stock Exchanges of Ireland.* Liverpool: Francis Cairns, 1986.

Tucker, Bernard. 'The Hibernian Patriot'. In *Jonathan Swift.* Dublin: Gill and Macmillan, 1983, pp. 61-86.

Tyrrell, W.E. *History of the Belfast Savings Bank.* Belfast: Committee of Management of the Belfast Savings Bank, 1946.

Whitaker, T.K. *Interests.* Dublin: Institute of Public Administration, 1983.

INDEX

Numerals in *italics* refer to additional text in margins (captions or definitions)

PICTURE ACKNOWLEDGEMENTS

Allied Irish Banks plc: pages 14 and 18

Bank of Ireland: page 31

Central Bank of Ireland: cover photograph and pages iii, 5 *(bottom)*, 46, 47, 49, 50, 54, 79 (reproduced with the kind permission of Michael and Justin Keating), 88, 94 and 96

Commission of the European Communities, Irish Office: pages 100 and 113

Commissioners of Public Works, Ireland: pages 2 *(bottom)* and 27

Mac Innes Photography Limited, with kind permission of The Irish Stock Exchange: page 66

National Museum of Ireland: pages 2 *(top)*, 4, 5 *(top)*, 8, 10 and 16.